FUNDAMENTALS OF
TEACHING AND LEARNING

FUNDAMENTALS OF TEACHING AND LEARNING

KAY F. QUAM

Nova Science Publishers, Inc.
Commack, New York

Editorial Production: Susan Boriotti
Office Manager: Annette Hellinger
Graphics: Frank Grucci and John T'Lustachowski
Information Editor: Tatiana Shohov
Book Production: Donna Dennis, Patrick Davin, Christine Mathosian, Tammy Sauter and Diane Sharp
Circulation: Maryanne Schmidt
Marketing/Sales: Cathy DeGregory

Library of Congress Cataloging-in-Publication Data

Quam, Kay F.
     Fundamentals of Teaching / by Kay F. Quam.
           p.   cm.
     Includes index.
     ISBN 1-56072-493-5. -- ISBN 1-56072-585-0 (pbk.)
     1. Teaching. 2. Learning.   I. Title.
LB1025.3.Q35   1998   98-19540
371.102—dc21   CIP

Printed in the United States of America

CONTENTS

INTRODUCTION

"No artist ever became successful without an enormous amount of rigorous training for his [sic] art, and continual submission to very tough criticism from his [sic] peers and mentors." (Miller, 1964).

I became a teacher accidentally. College did not prepare me for a career as a teacher, but as a nutrition expert. I stumbled into an opportunity to teach international cooking in the adult education program at the local community college. The experience was so rewarding, I was hooked as an educator. Because I was not formally prepared as a teacher, I learned how to teach through years of trial-and-error, by reading, and participating in seminars.

In the process, I discovered that there are better, faster, more efficient ways with few bad consequences. I also realized my experience was not unique. Thousands of people with expertise in specific subjects convey their knowledge to others without the benefit of a formal program for teachers. In addition to adult education instructors, there are doctors, nurses and related personnel in medical education, training directors in business and industry, and even professors in higher education.

My career developed into one of helping people learn to teach. This book is an introduction to how to teach. It can also be used by experienced teachers and trainers who want to transition into the newer model of education that encourages students' active participation.

This book is written as a compilation of my experiences acquired during a 20 year career of "teaching to teach." I acquired a collection of boxes in my basement containing clippings, articles, notes from training seminars and professional conferences, and little scraps of paper that I hung on to knowing someday they would all be useful when I wrote a book on learning to teach. In the process of organizing this book, I was reminded that my skills and ideas were influenced by numerous people and sources. My intent is to present my best collection of information, and several ideas are so best collection of information, and several ideas are so good, they are included even though the sources are unknown. I am grateful to all who inspired me, and have credited those I could verify.

My belief was always that some formal training on how to teach was necessary for teachers. Combining that training with the valuable wisdom gained from on-the-job experience leads to effective teaching. I continue to believe this even though my own experience of working with teachers often discounts this belief. Also, my dissertation research, How Family Physicians Learn to Teach Residents, revealed that advice for physicians who wanted to teach was just, "Go for it." This simple message suggested that in order to teach, no formal, systematic training is necessary. It reminds me today of the advertising message for athletes, "Just Do It." Certainly aspiring young athletes know that to excel, they must combine practice and training. No less can be expected of teachers.

After observations of many, many teachers, my current philosophy is that outstanding teachers dedicate themselves to a continuous process of erudition and praxis. Teachers certainly can learn to teach using their experience. This supports the Heuristic method of undertaking self-educating techniques to improve performance, trial-and-error methods, and experiential learning. However, a more formal, structured, systematic effort is needed and is beneficial.

My challenge in writing a book on effective teaching is to create one that will impact you and make a difference in your teaching. Let me suggest three ways to use this book.

1. Clearly, an independent, self-directed reading of the book is the first step. Each section is designed as a workbook so you can support your reading by completing the activities and applying the ideas. The value of reading is enhanced when you pursue the second approach.

2. One crystal clear revelation I have had from over 20 years of faculty development is that to improve teaching, teachers need to TALK about their teaching. It is not unlike the power of active learning, which espouses the concept of getting students to do something, and to think about what they are doing. This process also works for teaching.

I suggest that teachers form small groups to discuss the contents of this book. Each participant can take a chapter and facilitate a discussion on that topic. The facilitator need not to be an expert on the subject. The value of this format is that teachers can learn from each other through the process of talking, sharing experiences, and problem-solving. The book serves as a springboard for discussion.

3. The third method of using this book is that each major chapter can be presented as a structured training seminar. Included in each chapter is an outline or lesson plan (some are brief so you can gain skill at developing your own), and suggested ideas, activities, and exercises that can be used to foster group participation and application of the knowledge.

This book then is not intended as the "be all, end all" but rather as the impetus for teachers to get together and start talking about teaching. Once you involve yourself in this process of faculty development, my hope is that you will understand it not as a PANACEA, but recognize that it holds a PROMISE. The promise is that you can tune-up your teaching and improve your students' learning.

This book is organized around a model I developed to provide an answer to, when asked by people not formally prepared as educators, "Well, just what is it I need to know to teach?" The model includes both foundations (philosophy) and skills (practical).

FOUNDATIONS:

1. *Philosophical approaches* to education help teachers identify their personal philosophy of education and select teaching behaviors that reflect their beliefs and attitudes. The concept of *active learning* will be explored.

2. *Learning theories* and *adult learning principles* are discussed. These provide an understanding of why certain teaching techniques work.

3. Understanding the *teaching and learning process* includes definitions of teaching and learning, and ways to identify and adapt both *teaching styles and learning styles*.

4. Awareness of *characteristics of good teaching* helps teachers identify and develop those behaviors that allow them to function more effectively.

SKILLS:

1. The approach to instructional development begins with the process of *curriculum design* including objectives, content, planning, and preparing to teach.

2. Frequently used *teaching methods* are classified according to instructor-centered, interactive, individual, or experiential. Selecting teaching methods is explained. Advantages and disadvantages of various methods are explored.

3. Ideas on how to put power in your *presentations* and make an impact through *dynamic delivery* are presented.

4. Techniques for effectively *using audio visuals* to support teachers' content materials are presented.

5. *Evaluation* of teaching is a process of reflection with the emphasis on thinking about what was done and modifying future teaching. It involves both a look backward and a look ahead.

Pursuing development does not suggest that you are inadequate in your teaching. Professional development is rather a positive statement that you want to be the best you can be. I am reminded of the words below used to defend parents against those who would berate them for their child raising skills.

"You did what you knew how to do and when you knew better, you did better."
—Maya Angelou

Chapter 1

PROFESSIONAL DEVELOPMENT

"Good Teachers Never Stop Learning."

This section is approached using the standard format of a news story: Who, What, Where, When, Why and How. Let that journalism format guide you through this chapter, substituting teacher, trainer, or developer if you prefer.

WHO, WHAT, WHERE, WHEN, WHY AND HOW

WHO - The "Who" of professional development is YOU. Names used frequently to label those involved in the transfer of information include: teacher, trainer, faculty, preceptor, tutor, facilitator, leader, authority. The point is that development is for all of you and YOU are responsible for it. It is not something that someone else does to you.

Teachers are responsible to continually acquire new knowledge and skills to maintain their proficiency, and to willingly share the new knowledge and skills with others to enhance the effectiveness of the team. This underscores again why I feel they need to "talk about teaching" and through this sharing process, they can effect the overall quality of education in their institution or organization.

WHAT - Simply put, professional development is helping teachers learn what to do. And what they do is teach, provide service, research, and advise students. While orientation, development and skill building is essential in each of these four areas of faculty responsibility, this book focuses on the TEACH area of responsibility.

Professional development is a process that offers improvement in teaching abilities leading to increased knowledge and skills related to more effective teaching to enhance student learning. And that is the reason we teach - to help students learn.

Goals for development can be useful in defining what it strives to achieve. Professional development:

1. provides opportunities that improve the teaching/learning process.
2. is essential to initiate and support curricular change.
3. is a tool used to socialize faculty into the organizational philosophy. This often occurs during an initial process of orientation for faculty who are new to an organization. Development activities introduced during a change process or during any shifts in the mission of an institution, help reduce anxiety and resistance.
4. allows for changes in new techniques for effective teaching, but also requires changes in attitudes. Teachers need ways of thinking about teaching and learning as well as new skills and techniques.
5. provides a systematic way to keep current with developments in one's professional area.

There are three major categories of development. They are: Individual, Instructional, and Institutional. Examples of each include:

> **Individual** - Courses or activities in this category focus on individual growth and development, and self improvement of the person. Examples are retirement planning, time management and ways to raise self-esteem.
>
> **Institutional** - These programs are intended to improve the effectiveness of the organization and can include conflict management, team building, and change theory. Generally, when the administration proposes a new policy, or undertakes some form of development to comply with newly enacted legislation i.e. Americans with Disabilities Act (ADA), or sexual

harassment, development sessions are offered to help establish acceptance.

Instructional - These opportunities are designed to improve the process of instruction and can include designing curriculum, developing a lesson plan, using audio visuals, or leading group discussions.

All three categories are necessary to develop teachers. The priority given to each and the amount of time devoted will differ based on resources and goals of the organization. Faculty motivation may also impact the amount of time, energy, and effort devoted to each of the three categories.

WHERE - Professional development can occur anywhere. It can be an independent activity such as reading about teaching, which is a good way to start. Independent learning does not mean learning in isolation. Development is enhanced if the learning is applied to real situations or problems. Professional development takes place in an institution when small groups of faculty with common interests explore teaching effectiveness. Frequently, it occurs away from the parent organization, often in the form of attending a workshop, seminar, or professional meeting. One limitation of "going away" for development is that you come back full of enthusiasm and a renewed sense of excitement, but the environment you return to may not share that same feeling. There is little support for you to apply the skills you are so anxious to use in your home institution. When this happens, your energy and enthusiasm fizzles because your support team is missing. Surround yourself with people of like interests so you can support each other.

WHEN - As professionals, development is a continuous process. If we want students to be lifelong learners, then it is appropriate for teachers to model that same behavior. It is a continuous process, but various phases do take place in concert with the different goals expressed for faculty development. For example, new faculty may have both a more recognized need and more motivation early in their careers. New faculty are concerned that they master the content which reflects their subject matter expertise, and they often make content a priority over identifying and developing the skills of teaching they also need. Many faculty find it simply too overwhelming to concentrate on both. They focus on content because they can more quickly experience a high level of confidence. Once they master the content (at least until that current information becomes out of date) this frees them to pursue the skills and techniques of teaching. The challenge of actually understanding why the skills and techniques work, which they can discover through an exploration to uncover the attitudes and philosophies they hold about teaching, is recognized at a later time. At that point, faculty realize that their teaching behaviors are outward expressions of their philosophy and are closely connected.

WHY - Professional development espouses a philosophy of self-renewal, intellectual stimulation, and pragmatic skill development. Effective teaching requires continual upgrading of techniques and replenishing of the mind and spirit through development. Engaging in this process can bring new knowledge and inspiration to teaching and promote professional growth. Teachers often report a stronger sense of vitality when they keep current with teaching skills and content. It is evident there are many good reasons for professional development.

It may not be essential to first understand the importance of development before you engage in it. Rather, once you are engaged in activities that develop your teaching ability, the importance becomes evident to you. To provide a modicum of motivation, here are some reasons development is important for teachers.

1. Professional development is a stimulating, exciting process of renewal and helps sustain enthusiasm for teaching.
2. It is needed to accommodate changes in the learning process.
3. Student demographics have changed over the years to more heterogeneous groups.
4. Institutions are accountable to deliver a product/service for the dollars spent.
5. Institutions have a responsibility to ensure quality courses and quality instruction.
6. Knowledge is expanding so rapidly that teachers have a constant need to keep up-to-date, and a responsibility to experience professional growth through the process of learning.
7. Institutions are competing for students and good teaching attracts good students.
8. It is essential in tandem with curricular change.

HOW - Professional development comes in different sizes and shapes. Listed here are "Strategies to Improve Teaching."

1. Remain current with your content area.
2. Familiarize yourself with the literature on teaching effectiveness.
3. Become familiar with characteristics of good teaching described in Chapter 6.
4. Recall the good teachers you have had and emulate them.
5. Spend time in preparation. Information to assist you is in Chapter 7.
6. Identify a mentor who is willing to share experiences with you.
7. Seek the advice of colleagues by discussing teaching with them.
8. Observe other teachers in action. Why do we have peer review of our research, but not our teaching?
9. Ask colleagues to visit your class and offer suggestions for improvement or change.
10. Obtain feedback from your students. Some ways to do this are included in Chapter 15.
11. Videotape/audio tape your teaching and review by yourself or with others in positions to assist. This allows you to more clearly see yourself as others see and hear you.
12. Attend seminars designed to help improve teaching effectiveness. This action indicates strength, not weakness. However, attending is not enough. You must also do something which means taking action to change or do things differently.
13. Take a risk. You must be willing to experiment with the unknown, the uncomfortable, and the unfamiliar.
14. Work on communication, both listening and speaking. This is at the heart of interpersonal relationship skills. The relationship between teacher and student has a powerful impact on learning. Teaching is a human transaction. Technology can never replace the power of the relationship.
15. Participate in teaching exchanges, sabbaticals, and fellowships if an opportunity exists. The key to a successful sabbatical is to have a plan, not just using it as a haphazard time for reflection.

OVERCOMING RESISTANCE

So, after several pages of extolling the virtues of development, are you convinced of the necessity? Here are some reasons it may take more to convince you than what you have just read so far.

For the faculty developer charged with the task of providing development activities for teachers, there will be the frustration of resistance. To lessen this frustration, it is helpful to be clear on responsibility.

It is the institution's responsibility to provide the resources, the support, and the undisputed goal that faculty development is a priority and that it is important.

It is the responsibility of the faculty developer or trainer to provide opportunities, guidance, and make recommendations. To go beyond that is like trying to teach table manners to zoo animals. It cannot be done.

That is because it is the responsibility of the teacher to take advantage of the opportunities for growth and development. You must work at teaching effectiveness to improve student or trainee learning. No one else can do the work for you, and it will take work.

So, why do teachers resist? Here are some reasons.

1. Professional development at many institutions is unstructured and haphazard. The desultory nature causes teachers to question its value and often increases frustration and resistance.
2. Sufficient resources or commitment on the part of administration are lacking.
3. Time is limited. Teaching is a complex process that imposes many responsibilities competing for limited time. Lack of time is problematic when priorities are not established or are misplaced.
4. Lack of external reward. Research is financially rewarded more often than teaching in academic institutions, so effort is devoted to the area that pays off.
5. Inertia can cause faculty to be apathetic, especially after a long career of teaching that may foster stagnation.
6. Insecurity, lack of self-confidence, or ego involvement present stumbling blocks. Any threat of diminished self-worth can produce anxiety.

7. Lack of motivation is a determent to action. Teachers are motivated in different ways, including: Inner (Freud) Reward (Skinner) Growth (Rogers).

8. Teachers model the way they were taught. This strategy is recommended only if you model your teaching after a good teacher.

9. Good teaching is somewhat difficult to quantify. It is multidimensional, and characteristics that learners consider important are varied. Chapter 6 seeks to express tangible traits of teaching.

10. The institutional setting may not be receptive to change or to the introduction of new philosophies. This is often the case in introducing problem-based learning (PBL) when students are expected to be more responsible, which places teachers in roles other than authoritarian.

11. There is risk involved and concern over, "what if what I try doesn't work?"

12. The idea that "if it ain't broke, don't fix it."

13. The belief that good teachers are born, not made.

Faculty resist for all sorts of reasons. They resist by not availing themselves of the opportunities to improve. Woody Allen said, "Showing up is eighty percent of life." If teachers do not show up for development activities, it cannot be effective.

Because development cannot be successful without teacher involvement, that resistance needs to be turned into support.

All right. You are now convinced of the importance of professional development, and you are motivated to begin. So, what is holding you back? Here are some resources you will need to embark on your journey, and remember to take along your fellow travelers!

PROVIDING RESOURCES

1. Money to be used as rewards or for traveling to attend seminars and professional meetings.

2. Seminars presented by professionals.

3. Videotape equipment.

4. Audio visual support.

5. Professional observation by an educator or by your colleagues.
6. Other teachers to share in the development process.
7. Books.
8. A process for obtaining feedback from your students. Refer to Chapter 15 for guidance in this area.
9. Tools for self assessment, which are included in Chapter 6.

When you are the individual designated to coordinate, organize, or make possible development and training opportunities, here are some suggestions to help you experience success:

Get to know the people.

Reduce resistance, get involvement and solicit support.

Make participation voluntary, let everyone know they are welcome.

Work with the willing.

Offer a variety of opportunities.

Make your program structured, interactive, and rewarded.

Do not do it alone.

You are ready! You can determine what you want to know. This is based on some assessment of what things you already know and what skills you already possess, even though you may discover a need to tune-up some of them. Decide on specific areas and behaviors you want to examine and set a goal for improvement. Begin slowly.

Richard Bach, author of *Jonathan Livingston Seagull,* appropriately made this point when Jonathan was teaching Fletcher Gull some of the dynamics involved in improving his flying. As Jonathan explains it,

"The trick, Fletcher, is that we are trying to overcome our limitations in order, patiently. We do not tackle flying through rock until a little later in the program."

LESSON PLAN

Goal

To gain an overview perspective of professional development to aid your growth as a teacher.

Objectives:

To gain a broad understanding of what professional development is and its importance.

To develop an ongoing commitment to participate in development activities.

To increase awareness of what resources are available to assist you in your development.

Pre-Opening

Ask volunteers to state activities they do that are considered professional development.

Ask for a volunteer to record responses on the board or flip chart.

I. Introduction

State what you will cover, why it is important and what participants will know, think or be able to do at the end of the session.

II. Body

Discuss the Who, What, Where, Why, When, and How

Activities:

1. Brainstorm what causes some teachers (trainers, tutors) to resist development. Invite participants to share ideas for overcoming obstacles that interfere with their development to be more effective as teachers or trainers.

2. Conduct a force-field analysis. Have group identify forces that restrain or prevent them from professional development. Then identify forces that help (driving forces). Enlist a volunteer to stand in the center of an area to represent professional development. People from the group take on the role of each of

the forces. Ask people to position themselves in relation to the center person based on the strength of their force (i.e. the desire for growth could serve as a strong force, thereby standing close to the center individual). Restraining forces are on one side, driving forces on the opposite. When ways to reduce the restraining forces are identified by the group, new positions are taken, with the goal of all forces taking positions on the driving side. This activity affords participants a visual depiction and also allows them to become physically active.

III. Conclusion

Ask participants, "What one thing will you do as a result of this session on professional development?"

Verbally stating ideas gives everyone an opportunity to participate, it serves as a review, and it is also an action step toward applying the information gained.

Resources Needed: flip chart, marking pens, transparencies

WORKSHEET

What Is Professional Development?

List activities you have participated in during the last three years to help you as a teacher.

What did you gain from these activities?

List anything that keeps you from participating in professional development.

What are your development needs as a teacher?

State your goals for professional development during the next two years.

List resources you need. Place an asterisk by those that are not available.

What can be done to make the resources available?

Videotape yourself giving a presentation. What did you see that you did well?

What one thing could be more effective if done differently?

Chapter 2

FOUNDATIONS OF TEACHING AND LEARNING

"Knowledge exists to be imparted."

- Ralph Waldo Emerson

UNDERSTANDING TEACHING

To teach is to impart knowledge. Teaching is a process of structuring materials, providing information and demonstrating skills to students, and evaluating outcomes. The process requires an intellectual component necessary for content and also the ability to communicate the content. The overarching purpose of teaching is to produce discernible changes in student thinking, valuing, understanding, and development.

WHY TEACH?

"For me, teaching is a red-eye, sweaty-palm, sinking stomach profession. Red-eye, because I never feel ready to teach, no matter how late I stay up preparing the night before. Sweaty-palm, because I'm always nervous before I walk into that classroom, sure that I will be found out for the fool I am. Sinking stomach, because I walk out of the classroom an hour later convinced that I was even more boring than usual...["BUT,] I teach because it is a profession built on change...I like the freedom to make my own mistakes,...I like to ask questions...I like to learn...I teach best not what I know, but what I want to learn...I teach because, being around people who are beginning to breathe, I occasionally find myself catching my breath with them." (Beidler, 1984)

I have watched the movie *Educating Rita* (1984) many times and have always been moved by the power of the film. It is the story of a British hairdresser who attends the university, yearning to improve her life through education. Numerous principles of adults in learning situations are vividly depicted: barriers to learning, teacher-student relationships, and the value of acquiring an education. What I find the most moving is the final scene. At the airport, the professor turns and looks back at his former student as he boards the airplane. His eyes meet Rita's and she says, "Thanks." That is why I teach. When an exchange like this happens, the feeling that you have touched a student's life and he or she has touched yours, it has an extremely profound impact. What is significant is that it only takes one.

When I left one of my faculty development positions, faculty in a particular discipline had all been particularly receptive to my efforts to assist them in understanding the skills and philosophies of teaching and learning. Here is the poem they gave me:

There is a story that someone told about seeds being sowed on various places. We want you to know that a great many of the seeds which you have sowed with such dedication and skill have fallen on really fertile soil. They will continue to bear fruit not just in this place but in each of our lives wherever we may be because, to use another image, You have not just given us fish but you have taught us how to fish. In reality you have taught us how to plant seeds where we are too. We won't forget who taught us. Thank you!

I teach because of my mother, the teacher. Her pupils were in a one-room school house in Minnesota in 1940. When she died in 1995, two of her pupils from 55 years earlier, attended her funeral service. One remembered her saying, "She was my 7th grade teacher and in all sincerity, she was my favorite teacher." To make such an impression on someone is an important task and is a lasting tribute.

It is imperative for you as a teacher to find a compelling answer to "Why teach?" This process of introspection is necessary and can be affirming. The answer gives rise to a teaching philosophy, increases self-confidence, and establishes a long term commitment to the profession. If not, you can experience tedium and early burnout.

The best teachers, trainers, or facilitators are those who embrace their profession as a personal thing. It is not awarded, or inherited, and it does not come as a result of education alone. Only those who put together their knowledge and skill, with all their ability and exhibit a complete dedication of purpose, are truly professionals.

EDUCATIONAL PHILOSOPHY

As educators we engage in the daily tasks associated with teaching without understanding the theories and philosophies that bring meaning and direction to our teaching. We are concerned with improving the skills and techniques, rather than becoming aware of the principles. Our focus is on the details rather than on seeing the big picture.

Our educational attitudes and philosophies do effect teaching behaviors. Knowles (1970) says new attitudes are needed; acquiring new techniques alone is not sufficient Philosophy is a collection of beliefs: beliefs about the student, the teacher, and the process of teaching and learning. Philosophy must be consistent with one's practice. The behaviors become the concrete, visible expression of the abstract philosophy.

Teachers tend to model educational philosophy with behaviors that reflect their beliefs. Elias and Merriam (1980) stated the difference between those practicing a profession and a "professional" is awareness of the factors behind their behaviors.

Brookfield (1990) stated, "However, to emphasize either the plurality of teaching methods or the essentially artistic nature of teaching is to obscure the central question of what should be the purpose of teaching. There may indeed be a plurality of methods available for the achievement of a particular goal, and the pursuit of that goal and the use of these methods may indeed require art. But this does not remove the necessity of developing a clear philosophical rationale to guide practice. Educational philosophy is translated into operational behaviors that become apparent in the classroom practices." He further states, "the danger arises when the teacher is unaware of any philosophical rationale underlying his or her activities."

Jerold Apps (Flanner and Wistock, 1991) notes, "A crucial point is reached when an educator begins to raise questions about what he or she does, why he or she does it, and what this activity should consist of. These considerations lie at the heart of a working philosophy." To began to identify and develop one's working philosophy, three steps are involved:

1)   be aware of one's philosophy - examine what you do and search for the "why"
2)   engage in ongoing evaluation
3)   reflect on how philosophy is carried out in practice

Five suggestions for conducting on-going evaluation are encouraged by Flanner and Wistock (1991):

1. self-reflection about the strengths and weaknesses of our philosophy
2. look at others and make comparisons - read the literature and talk with others about beliefs
3. examine the strengths of your beliefs
4. consider organizational setting in which you work - is your style compatible with the organization's philosophy?
5. write it down--this will clarify and focus your thoughts

Be prepared to regularly examine beliefs and how these beliefs influence your practice. Strive for a strong nexus between your philosophy and your behaviors. This then is truly an on-going process that enables you to jettison those behaviors no longer consistent with your philosophy.

Philosophy is an abstract concept and as such, is difficult to explain in concrete terms. To assist educators in identifying a personal philosophy of education, Zinn (1983) developed and validated a self-assessment tool, the Philosophy of Adult Education Inventory (PAEI)©. This inventory asks you as an educator, about everyday decisions and choices you make in planning educational activities. There are fifteen sentence stems on the Inventory, each of which has five different completion statement options. The five options are representative of five prevailing philosophies of the field of adult education, as originally identified by Elias and Merriam in 1980. (1995, 2nd. ed.). They are Liberal (arts), Behavioral, Progressive, Humanistic, and Radical. They are shown in matrix form on page 35. The matrix includes purpose(s) of adult education, characteristics of adult learners, teacher's role, key concepts and teaching methods, and people and practices most representative of each philosophy.

When the Inventory is completed, "scores" are transferred to a Scoring Matrix to show how closely the respondent's personal philosophical orientation is aligned with the five philosophies. The highest score reflects which of the five philosophies is closest to your own beliefs, and the lowest score is the one least like yours.

The Inventory appears on page 20 and is reproduced for one-time use only. Additional copies may be ordered from Dr. Zinn at: Lifelong Learning Options, 4757 West Moorhead Circle, Boulder, CO 80303.

Another instrument to help educators identify orientations about education is Hadley's Educational Orientation Questionnaire (EOQ) (1975). It consists of 60 statements. Responses provide an indication if your views are pedagogical (child) or andragogical (adult). That questionnaire appears on page 36 and is intended for one-time personal assessment only. Additional use of the questionnaire may be negotiated with Dr. Herschel Hadley, 45 Martin St., Acton, MA 01720.

The following philosophies appeared in a monograph "In Celebration of Teaching: Reflections of University of Hawaii Professors." (Center for Teaching Excellence, 1991).

Ann Bayer – Dept. of Curriculum and Instruction. What I find so fascinating about teaching is that I'm still learning how to do it. I realize that I learned as much from my students as they did from me. What worked was having the students actively involved in their learning. They seemed to be more engaged if the tasks held some meaning for them, and if they could use their peers as resources. Students take increasing responsibility for their own learning.

Fred Creager - School of Architecture. The role of a teacher is to stimulate and challenge the student to excel. As an external stimulus is introduced into the oyster to develop the pearl, so a teacher acts to develop the students' knowledge and skills.

Thomas Jackson - Dept. of Philosophy. The Socratic notion of "teacher as midwife," with appropriate clarifications, is a model that holds great power for me. I think it is both my love of people and the joy and energy that comes from being able to draw others into the discovery of new ideas and the power of one's own mind, as this unfolds in situations that are intellectually safe, that reflect who I am as a person, and what keeps me fulfilled in the teaching profession.

Laurence Jacobs - Dept. of Marketing. My general approach to teaching is to view each class as a unique situation. I ask myself one question: What is the best way to gain student involvement? How can I get them to appreciate the subject matter? What are the ideas which are most important for an understanding of the subject matter? How can these key concepts be demonstrated in a way which is relevant and meaningful to the student?

Karen Jolly - Dept. of History. As I have examined why I am in this profession, and what I hope to accomplish, I have concluded that teaching is is in many ways a gift--the gift or desire to create understanding in someone else. Consequently, teaching involves not only knowing the subject, but also knowing the students and where they are coming from in order to effectively communicate the material to them.

Cheryl Matsumoto - School of Accountancy. My philosophy of teaching can best be summed up in the following words of William Purkey: "The student's motor is always running. The function of the educator is to place the signs, build the roads, direct the traffic and teach good driving -- but not drive the car." This quotation indicates to me that educators are the facilitators or directors of education. As facilitator, we may learn ourselves, but we cannot expect to learn for our students.

WHAT IS LEARNING?

It is a change in human disposition or capability which can be retained and is not related to growth. For example, around the age of 12-14 months, children start to walk. This however, is not something they really learn, but rather is the taking on of tasks associated with their growth. These tasks occur at somewhat predetermined and scheduled intervals throughout their lives. It is a process within which a person manifests different traits that have been carried in his/her cells since conception.

Most human behaviors are not linked to instinct, but rather, must be learned. Unlike animals, who are "hard wired" at birth, humans are given the capacity to learn. Learning is an experience which occurs inside the learner and is activated by the learner. Learning is the discovery of personal meaning and worth of ideas. It is a change in insights, behaviors, perceptions, or motivation or a combination of these things. Learning is also a consequence of experience.

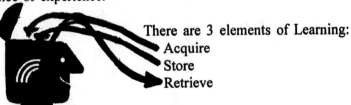

There are 3 elements of Learning:
Acquire
Store
Retrieve

Figure 2: Elements of Learning

Learning occurs in the three domains of cognitive, affective, and psychomotor. The outcomes of learning in each domain are:

a) Cognitive - thinking skills - also includes acquiring verbal information to learn facts and concepts and intellectual learning for knowledge
b) Affective - attitudes, beliefs and values
c) Psychomotor - skills to perform tasks

One key to successful learning is engagement. To be engaged, students must perceive the need for a transaction to occur. The transaction occurs between the four elements of learner, teacher, goal, and the process involved to achieve the goal. Teaching and learning is a human process with shared responsibilities.

Behind every great teacher is a great philosophy. The way you teach is explained by your philosophy. It describes what you believe in and exposes your values. While it is an integral part of your teaching self, it is malleable, and subject to continual evaluation and reshaping. Embrace the idea that teaching requires certain skills, and that it is equally important to understand theories and principles that govern our teaching.

Teaching and learning are not separate entities. One does not suggest what the teacher does and the other what the student does. Education is a combination of both. Gaining an understanding of what teaching and learning are and seeing how intertwined they are helps form and shape your philosophical approach to the education process.

> "A man was walking in the desert when a voice said to him, 'Pick up some pebbles and put them in your pocket, and tomorrow you will be both sorry and glad.'
>
> The man obeyed. He stooped down and picked up a handful of pebbles and put them in his pocket. The next morning he reached into his pocket and found diamonds and rubies and emeralds. And he was both glad and sorry. Glad that he had taken some--sorry that he hadn't taken more. And so it is with education."
>
> - William Cunningham

PHILOSOPHY OF ADULT EDUCATION INVENTORY (REVISED, 1994)

The Philosophy of Adult Education Inventory© (PAEI) is an assessment instrument developed to assist the adult educator to identify his/her personal philosophy of education and to compare it with prevailing philosophies in the field of adult education. The PAEI© was designed to be self-administered, self-scored and self-interpreter.

Validity and reliability test data are summarized in *Dissertation Abstracts International*, 44, 1667A-1668A (Zinn, 1983).

Copyright 1994 by Lorraine M. Zinn. All rights reserved. This material is not to be copied or disseminated without permission. Additional copies may be ordered from Lifelong Learning Options, 4757 West Moorhead Circle, Boulder, CO 80303-6157 or FAX 303-499-7341.

PHILOSOPHY OF ADULT EDUCATION INVENTORY (REV. 1994)
INSTRUCTIONS FOR COMPLETION

Each of the fifteen (15) items on the inventory begins with an incomplete sentence, followed by five different options that might complete the sentence. Underneath each option is a scale from 1 to 7, followed by a small letter in parentheses. For the present, ignore the letters; use only the numbers on the scale.

To complete the Inventory, read each sentence stem and each optional phrase that completes it. On the 1-7 scale, CIRCLE the number that most closely indicates how you feel about each option. The scale goes from 1 (strongly disagree) to 7 (strongly agree), with a neutral point, (4) if you don't have any opinion or aren't sure about a particular option.

Continue through all the items, reading the sentence stem and indicating how strongly you agree or disagree with each of the options. Please respond to every option, even if you feel neutral about it. THERE ARE NO RIGHT OR WRONG ANSWERS!

As you go through the Inventory, respond according to what you most frequently or most likely do. If it helps you to respond more easily, you may want to focus on a specific course that you teach. If you do focus on a particular course, choose one that you feel most comfortable teaching – one that you think best reflects your preferred style of teaching.

HAVE FUN!

STRONGLY DISAGREE			NEUTRAL			STRONGLY AGREE
1	2	3	4	5	6	7

1. IN PLANNING AN EDUCATIONAL ACTIVITY, I AM MOST LIKELY TO:

Identify, in conjunction with learners, significant social, cultural, and/or political issues and plan learning activities around them.

1	2	3	4	5	6	7(h)

Clearly identify the results I want and develop a program, class, workshop, etc. that will achieve those results.

1	2	3	4	5	6	7(c)

Begin with a lesson plan that organizes what I plan to teach, when and how.

1	2	3	4	5	6	7(a)

Assess learners' needs and develop valid learning activities based on those needs.

1	2	3	4	5	6	7(d)

Consider the areas of greatest interest to the learners and plan to deal with them, regardless of what they may be.

1	2	3	4	5	6	7(f)

2. PEOPLE LEARN BEST:

When the new knowledge is presented from a problem-solving approach.

1	2	3	4	5	6	7(x)

When the learning activity is clearly structured and provides for practice and repetition.

1   2   3   4   5   6   7(w)

Through discussion with other learners and a group coordinator.

1   2   3   4   5   6   7(z)

When they are free to explore, without the constraints of a "system."

1   2   3   4   5   6   7(y)

From an "expert" who knows what he or she is talking about.

1   2   3   4   5   6   7(v)

3. THE PRIMARY PURPOSE OF ADULT EDUCATION IS:

To facilitate personal development on the part of the learner.

1   2   3   4   5   6   7(f)

To increase learners' awareness of the need for social change and to enable them to effect such change.

1   2   3   4   5   6   7(h)

To increase knowledge and develop conceptual or theoretical understanding.

1   2   3   4   5   6   7(a)

To establish the learners' capacity to solve everyday problems.

1   2   3   4   5   6   7(d)

To develop the learners' competency and mastery of specific knowledge and skills.

1   2   3   4   5   6   7(c)

4. MOST OF WHAT PEOPLE KNOW:

Is a result of consciously pursuing their goals, solving problems as they go.

| 1 | 2 | 3 | 4 | 5 | 6 | 7(x) |

They have learned through critical or reflective thinking focused on important social, cultural, and/or political issues.

| 1 | 2 | 3 | 4 | 5 | 6 | 7(z) |

They have learned through a trial-and-feedback process.

| 1 | 2 | 3 | 4 | 5 | 6 | 7(w) |

They have gained through self-discovery rather than some "teaching" process.

| 1 | 2 | 3 | 4 | 5 | 6 | 7(y) |

They have acquired through a systematic and comprehensive educational process.

| 1 | 2 | 3 | 4 | 5 | 6 | 7(v) |

5. DECISIONS ABOUT WHAT TO INCLUDE IN A LEARNING ACTIVITY;

Should be made mostly by the learner in consultation with a facilitator.

| 1 | 2 | 3 | 4 | 5 | 6 | 7(f) |

Should be based on what learners know and what the teacher believes they should know at the end of the activity.

| 1 | 2 | 3 | 4 | 5 | 6 | 7(c) |

Should be based on a consideration of key social, political, economic, and/or cultural situations.

| 1 | 2 | 3 | 4 | 5 | 6 | 7(h) |

Should be based on a consideration of the learners' needs, interests, and problems.

| 1 | 2 | 3 | 4 | 5 | 6 | 7(d) |

Should be based on careful analysis by the teacher of the material to be covered and the concepts to be taught.

1   2   3   4   5   6   7 (a)

6. GOOD ADULT EDUCATORS START PLANNING INSTRUCTION:

By considering the specific outcomes they are looking for an the most efficient ways of producing them in learners.

1   2   3   4   5   6   7 (w)

By identifying everyday problems that can be solved as a result of the instruction.

1   2   3   4   5   6   7 (x)

By clarifying the content, concepts, and/or theoretical principles to be taught.

1   2   3   4   5   6   7 (v)

By clarifying key social, cultural, economic, and/or political issues that affect the lives of the learners.

1   2   3   4   5   6   7 (z)

By asking learners to identify what they want to learn and how they want to learn it.

1   2   3   4   5   6   7 (y)

7. AS AN ADULT EDUCATOR, I AM MOST SUCCESSFUL IN SITUATIONS:

That are unstructured and flexible enough to follow learners' interests.

1   2   3   4   5   6   7 (f)

That are fairly structured, with clear learning objectives and built-in feedback to the learners.

1   2   3   4   5   6   7 (c)

Where I can focus on practical skills and knowledge that can put to use in solving problems.

| 1 | 2 | 3 | 4 | 5 | 6 | 7 (d) |

Where the scope of the new material is fairly clear and the subject matter is logically organized.

| 1 | 2 | 3 | 4 | 5 | 6 | 7 (a) |

Where the learners have some awareness of social, cultural, economic and political issues and are willing to explore the impact of such issues on their daily lives.

| 1 | 2 | 3 | 4 | 5 | 6 | 7 (h) |

8. IN PLANNING AN EDUCATIONAL ACTIVITY, I TRY TO CREATE:

The real world – problems and all – and to develop learners' capacities for dealing with it.

| 1 | 2 | 3 | 4 | 5 | 6 | 7 (x) |

A setting in which learners are encouraged to examine their beliefs and values and to raise critical questions.

| 1 | 2 | 3 | 4 | 5 | 6 | 7 (z) |

A controlled environment that attracts and holds the learners, moving them systematically towards the objectives.

| 1 | 2 | 3 | 4 | 5 | 6 | 7 (w) |

A clear outline of the content and the concepts to be taught.

| 1 | 2 | 3 | 4 | 5 | 6 | 7 (v) |

A supportive climate that facilitates self-discovery and interaction.

| 1 | 2 | 3 | 4 | 5 | 6 | 7 (y) |

9. THE LEARNERS' FEELINGS DURING THE LEARNING PROCESS:

Must be brought to the surface in order for learners to become truly involved in their learning.

1   2   3   4   5   6   7 (h)

Provide energy that can be focused on problems or questions.

1   2   3   4   5   6   7 (d)

Will probably have a great deal to do with the way they approach their learning.

1   2   3   4   5   6   7 (f)

Are used by the skillful adult educator to accomplish the learning objectives.

1   2   3   4   5   6   7 (c)

Are likely to get in the way of teaching and learning by diverting the learners' attention.

1   2   3   4   5   6   7 (a)

10. THE TEACHING METHODS I PREFER TO USE:

Focus on problem-solving and present real challenges to the learner.

1   2   3   4   5   6   7 (x)

Emphasize practice and feedback to the learner.

1   2   3   4   5   6   7 (w)

Are mostly non-directive, encouraging the learner to take responsibility for his/her own learning.

1   2   3   4   5   6   7 (y)

Involve learners in discussion and critical examination of controversial issues.

1   2   3   4   5   6   7 (z)

Are determined primarily by the subject or content to be covered.

1   2   3   4   5   6   7 (v)

11. WHEN LEARNERS ARE UNINTERESTED IN A SUBJECT, IT IS PROBABLY BECAUSE:

They do not realize how serious the consequences of not understanding or not learning the subject may be.

1   2   3   4   5   6   7 (h)

They do not see any benefit for their daily lives.

1   2   3   4   5   6   7 (d)

The teacher does not know enough about the subject or is unable to make it interesting to the learner.

1   2   3   4   5   6   7 (a)

They are not getting adequate practice or feedback during the learning process.

1   2   3   4   5   6   7 (c)

They are not ready to learn it or it is not a high priority for them personally.

1   2   3   4   5   6   7 (f)

12. DIFFERENCES AMONG ADULT LEARNERS:

Are relatively unimportant as long as the learners gain a common base of understanding through the learning experience.

1   2   3   4   5   6   7 (v)

Enable them to learn best on their own time and in their own way.

1   2   3   4   5   6   7 (y)

Are primarily due to differences in their life experiences and will usually lead them to make different applications of new knowledge and skills to their own situations.

1   2   3   4   5   6   7 (x)

Arise from their particular cultural and social situations and should *not* be minimized even as they recognize common needs and problems.

1   2   3   4   5   6   7 (z)

Will not interfere with their learning if each learner is given adequate opportunity for practice and reinforcement.

1   2   3   4   5   6   7 (w)

13. EVALUATION OF LEARNING OUTCOMES:

Is not of great importance and may not be possible, because the impact of learning may not be evident until much later.

1   2   3   4   5   6   7 (h)

Should be built into the system, so that learners will continually receive feedback and can adjust their performance accordingly.

1   2   3   4   5   6   7 (c)

Is best done by the learners themselves, for their own purposes.

1   2   3   4   5   6   7 (f)

Lets the teacher know how much learners have increased their knowledge and conceptual understanding of new material.
1   2   3   4   5   6   7 (a)

Is best accomplished when the learner encounters a problem, either in the learning setting or the real world, and successfully resolves it.

1   2   3   4   5   6   7 (d)

14. MY PRIMARY ROLE AS A TEACHER OF ADULTS IS TO:

Guide learners through structured learning activities with well-directed feedback.

1   2   3   4   5   6   7 (w)

Systematically lead learners in acquiring new information and understanding underlying theories and concepts.

1   2   3   4   5   6   7 (v)

Help learners identify and solve problems better.

1   2   3   4   5   6   7 (x)

Increase learners' awareness of social, cultural, economic, and/or political issues and help them learn how to have an impact on these situations.

1   2   3   4   5   6   7 (z)

Facilitate, but not to direct, learning activities.

1   2   3   4   5   6   7 (y)

15. IN THE END, IF LEARNERS HAVE NOT LEARNED WHAT WAS TAUGHT:

The teacher has not actually "taught."

1   2   3   4   5   6   7 (a)

They need to repeat the experience, or a portion of it.

1   2   3   4   5   6   7 (c)

They may have learned something else that they consider just as interesting or useful.

| 1 | 2 | 3 | 4 | 5 | 6 | 7 (f) |

They do not realize how learning will enable them to significantly influence society.

| 1 | 2 | 3 | 4 | 5 | 6 | 7 (h) |

It is probably because they are unable to make practical application of new knowledge to problems in their daily lives.

| 1 | 2 | 3 | 4 | 5 | 6 | 7 (d) |

SCORING INSTRUCTIONS

After completing the Inventory, go back to your responses and find the small letter in parentheses to the far right of each rating scale. This is a code letter for scoring the Inventory. Transfer each of your numbers from the rating scales to the SCORING MATRIX in the right-hand column. For example, for item #1, if you circled a 5 for option (a), write the number 5 in the box for 1(a). Note that item #1 has five different responses: a, c, d, f, h. *Record all five of your responses for item #1*, then continue with #2-#15 (which also have five different responses each). When you finish, there will be numbers in *every other square* in the SCORING MATRIX (like a checkerboard).

YOUR TOTAL SCORES

Now, add all the numbers by columns, from top to bottom, so you have *ten* separate subtotals. None of these subtotals should be higher than 56; nor should any be lower than 7. For TOTAL SCORES, combine the subtotals from the columns on the Scoring Matrix, as indicated below. Note: TOTAL SCORES should be no higher than 105, nor lower than 15.

L(a+v)= _____   B(c+w)= _____   P(d+x)= _____

(H(f+y)= _____   R(h+z)= _____

Philosophy of Adult Education©
SCORING MATRIX

ITEM	c	w	a	v	d	x	f	y	h	z
1										
2										
3										
4										
5										
6										
7										
8										
9										
10										
11										
12										
13										
14										
15										
SUB-TOTALS										
ADD	c + w		a + v		d + x		f + y		h + z	
YOUR SCORES	B =		C =		P =		H =		S =	

What Your Scores Indicate

L = LIBERAL (ARTS) ADULT EDUCATION
(Education for Intellectual Development; General Education for Life)

B = BEHAVIORAL ADULT EDUCATION
(Education for Competence, Behavioral Change, Compliance with Standards)

P = PROGRESSIVE ADULT EDUCATION
(Education for Practical Problem Solving)

H = HUMANISTIC ADULT EDUCATION
(Education for Individual Self-Actualization)

R = RADICAL ADULT EDUCATION
(Education for Transforming Society)

What is a Philosophy of Education?

A Philosophy of Education represents a comprehensive and interrelated set of values and beliefs as applied to education – including beliefs about the purpose and nature of human life, the role of the individual in society, purposes or goals of education, role(s) of teachers and students, important subject matter, and effective teaching approaches.

An educational philosophy is much broader than a preference for specific teaching methods – although *preferred* teaching techniques are usually consistent with the educational philosophy. However, teaching techniques most characteristic of one philosophy may be used selectively by a teacher who has a *different* educational philosophy. Educational philosophies are fairly deeply held, closely aligned with people's life values, and unlikely to change significantly. Teaching *techniques* or *teaching style*, however, may vary depending on what works best in a particular situation, as long as the techniques used are not incompatible with basic premises of a teacher's philosophy of education.

On the next page, you will find brief descriptions of these five Philosophies of Adult Education.* You may want to write your score for each Philosophy above the column that describes it. Your *highest* score reflects the Philosophy that is *closest* to your own beliefs; your *lowest* score reflects

---

* Descriptions adapted from J. Elias and S. Merriam (1995), *Philosophical Foundations of Adult Education* (2nd. ed.), Krieger.

a Philosophy that is *least* like yours. For example, a score of 90-105 indicates that you very strongly agree with that Philosophy; a score of 25 or lower indicates that you very strongly disagree with a given Philosophy. NOTE: If you find your scores fairly equal among all of the Philosophies, or spread among three or more, you may want to spend some time further clarifying your beliefs and values and looking for possible contradictions among them.

Most Adult Educators have a clear primary philosophical orientation, or share two that are stronger than others. Typical combinations are: *LIBERAL (ARTS)* and *BEHAVIORAL, PROGRESSIVE* and *HUMANISTIC, PROGRESSIVE* and *RADICAL,* or HUMANISTIC and *RADICAL.* On the other hand, it is quite *unlikely* that you would have high scores in both *Liberal (ARTS)* and *RADICAL,* or *BEHAVIORAL* and *HUMANISTIC* Philosophies. These philosophies have key underlying assumptions that are inherently contradictory. (For example, the primary purpose of Behavioral Education is to ensure compliance with expectations or standards set by others; while Humanistic Education is intended to enhance individual self-development – which may or may not meet anyone else's expectations or standards.)

There is no *right* or *wrong* Philosophy of Adult Education. The Philosophy of Adult Education Inventory© is designed to reflect back to you some of your own beliefs, not to make judgments about those beliefs. It is up to you to decide how your beliefs may influence your decisions and actions as an educator, and how your personal educational philosophy may be well-suited, or perhaps not the best match, for the educational setting in which you work.

FIVE PHILOSOPHIES OF ADULT EDUCATION

TOTAL SCORES	L=___	B=___	P=___	H=___	R=___
	LIBERAL (ARTS) ADULT EDUCATION	BEHAVIORAL ADULT EDUCATION	PROGRESSIVE ADULT EDUCATION	HUMANISTIC ADULT EDUCATION	RADICAL ADULT EDUCATIONAL
PURPOSE(S)	To develop intellectual powers of the mind; to enhance the broadest sense of learning; to provide a general, "well-rounded" education.	To promote competence, skill development and behavioral change; ensure compliance with standards and societal expectations.	To support responsible participation in society; to give learners practical knowledge and problem-solving skills.	To enhance personal growth and development; to facilitate individual self-actualization.	To bring about, through education, fundamental social, cultural, political, and economic changes in society.
LEARNER(S)	"Renaissance person"; always a learner, seeks knowledge; expected to gain and conceptual and theoretical understanding.	Learners not involved in setting objectives; master one step before another; practice behaviors/skills to get them right.	Learner needs, interests, and experiences are valued and become part of learning process; learner takes an active role in learning.	Learner is highly motivated and self-directed; assumes responsibility for learning; very involved in planning learning projects.	Learner and "teacher" are equal in learning process; personal autonomy; learner is empowered; voluntary participated.
TEACHER ROLE	The "expert"; transmitter of knowledge; teaches students to think; clearly directs learning process.	Manager, controller, authoritative; sets expectations; predicts and directs learning outcomes.	Organizer; guides learning process; provides real-life learning applications; helps learners work cooperatively.	Facilitator; helper, mutual participant in teaching-learning exchange; supports learning process.	Coordinator; convener, equal partner with learner, suggests but does not determine directions.

Foundations of Teaching and Learning

CONCEPTS/ KEY WORDS	Liberal arts; learning for its own sake; general and comprehensive education; critical thinking; traditional knowledge; academic excellence.	Standards-based; mastery learning; competence; behavioral objectives; performance; practice, feedback/reinforcement; accountability.	Problem-solving; practical learning; experience-based; needs assessment; transfer of learning; active inquiry; collaboration; social responsibility.	Freedom; autonomy; individuality; teaching-learning exchange; self-directedness; interpersonal communication; openness; authenticity; feelings.	Consciousness-raising; praxis; noncompulsory learning; autonomy; social action; empowerment; social justice; commitment; transformation.
METHODS	Lecture; reading and critical analysis; question-and-answer; teacher-led discussion; individual study; standardized testing.	Computer-based instruction, lock-step curriculum, skill training, demo & practice, criterion-referenced testing.	Projects; scientific or experimental method; simulations; group investigation; cooperative learning; portfolios.	Experimental learning; discovery learning; open discussion; individual projects; collaborative learning; independent study; self-assessment.	Critical discussion and reflection; problem-posing; analysis of media output; social action theater.
PEOPLE & PRACTICES	Aristotle, Plato, Adler, Rousseau, Piaget, Houle, Great Books Society, Paideia Program, Center for the Study of Liberal Education, Chautauqua, Elderhostel.	Thorndike, Watson, Skinner, Tyler, Mager, vocational training, management-by-objectives, certification exams, military training, religious indoctrination.	Dewey, Whitehead, Lindeman, community college developmental studies, citizenship education, cooperative extension, university without walls, community schools.	Rogers, Maslow, Knowles, Tough, group dynamics, self-directed learning, I'm OK, You're OK; diversity education, credit for prior learning.	Holt, Freire, Illich, Kozol, Shor, Ohliger, Perelman, free school movement, Afro-centrism, voter registration/education, social justice education.

L.M. Zinn, PAE1© Rev. 1994. Used with permission.

EDUCATIONAL ORIENTATION QUESTIONNAIRE

Name _____

Address _____

Below are statements about education, teaching, and learning. These have been chosen to express several different viewpoints.

Please note: In completing this questionnaire keep in mind that the word "student" means adult student, and the word "teacher" means yourself – the person filling out the questionnaire. In other words, your answers indicate your educational orientation in working with adults.

For *each* statement, please put an "X" in one of the five boxes in front of that statement. Choose the box that indicates your attitude or position best – how much you agree or disagree with that statement. The five positions from which to choose are:

SA – I strongly agree with this statement.
A – I agree with this statement.
U – I'm too uncertain about this statement to agree or disagree.
D – I disagree with this statement.
SD – I strongly disagree with this statement.

SA A U D SD
( )( )( )( )( ) 1. Education should focus on what is sure, reliable, and lasting.
( )( )( )( )( ) 2. Teaching effectiveness should be measured by students' increase in examination of their own feelings, attitudes, and behaviors.
( )( )( )( )( ) 3. Students need a strong teacher who can direct their learning.
( )( )( )( )( ) 4. It's hard to keep people from learning.
( )( )( )( )( ) 5. Learning is an intellectual process of understanding ideas (concepts) and acquiring skills.

SA A U D SD
( )( )( )( )( ) 6. Effective learning occurs most often when students actively participate in deciding what is to be learned and how.

( )( )( )( )( ) 7. Giving examinations regularly motivates students to learn.

( )( )( )( )( ) 8. Organization of the content and sequence of learning activities should grow out of students' needs, with their participation.

( )( )( )( )( ) 9. It should be the teacher's responsibility to evaluate students' achievements and assign grades.

( )( )( )( )( ) 10. The best sources of ideas for improving teaching and education are the students.

SA   A   U   D   SD

( )( )( )( )( ) 11. Competition among students encourages keen learning.

( )( )( )( )( ) 12. A teacher by his behavior should show each student that his abilities and experiences are respected and valued.

( )( )( )( )( ) 13. A teacher should help students accept values of our society.

( )( )( )( )( ) 14. To see education as transmittal of knowledge is obsolete.

( )( )( )( )( ) 15. Students tend to be much alike.

( )( )( )( )( ) 16. It is a teacher's responsibility to motivate students to learn what they ought to learn.

SA   A   U   D   SD   17. Clear explanation by the teacher is essential for effective learning.

( )( )( )( )( ) 18. A teacher's primary responsibility is helping students choose and develop their own directions for learning.

( )( )( )( )( ) 19. A good teacher makes the decisions about what should be taught, when, and how.

( )( )( )( )( ) 20. A teacher seldom needs to know the average students as separate individuals.

( )( )( )( )( ) 21. A teacher should not change his expressed decisions without unusually good reasons.

SA   A   U   D   SD

( )( )( )( )( ) 22. Emphasizing efficiency in teaching often blocks development of an effective learning climate.

( )( )( )( )( ) 23. An adult education program should be evaluated by the same standards as other accredited programs of education.

( )( )( )( )( ) 24. Evaluating his achievement should be primarily a responsibility of the student since he has the necessary data.

( )( )( )( )( )25.   Competition among students develops conceit, selfishness, and envy.

( )( )( )( )( )26.   A teacher should discuss his blunders and learnings with students.

SA   A   U   D   SD

( )( )( )( )( )27.   A teacher should be sure his questions steer students toward truth.

( )( )( )( )( )28.   Educational objectives should define changes in behavior which the student desires and the teacher helps him undertake.

( )( )( )( )( )29.   Most students are able to keep their emotions under good control.

( )( )( )( )( )30.   Students are quite competent to choose and carry out their own projects for learning.

( )( )( )( )( )31.   A teacher should help students free themselves of fixed habits and patterns of thought that block their growth.

SA   A   U   D   SD

( )( )( )( )( )32.   The major qualifications of a teacher are grasp of subject matter and ability to explain (demonstrate) it clearly and interestingly.

( )( )( )( )( )33.   It is better for students to create their own learning activities and materials than for the teacher to provide them.

( )( )( )( )( )34.   A teacher should require assignments and grade them.

( )( )( )( )( )35.   Use of a topical outline course plan often blocks a teacher's perception of students' needs.

( )( )( )( )( )36.   An adult education program should be evaluated only in terms of its own objectives.

SA   A   U   D   SD

( )( )( )( )( )37.   Competition among students develops courage, determination, and industry.

( )( )( )( )( )38.   A teacher should provide opportunities for warm relationships with students and among students.

SA   A   U   D   SD

( )( )( )( )( )39.   Education should lead people to goals that result in orderly, reasonable lives.

( )( )( )( )( )40.   Education should increase students' critical evaluation of our society and courage to try new, creative, satisfying behavior.

( )( )( )( )( )41.   Often students don't know what is best for them.

( )( )( )( )( )42. When a teacher makes a mistake, he is likely to lose students' respect.

( )( )( )( )( )43. Maturity depends more on continuing growth in self-understanding than on growth in knowledge.

SA   A   U   D   SD

( )( )( )( )( )44. Students frequently "get off the subject" either intentionally or unintentionally.

( )( )( )( )( )45. Education programs which tell what should be learned and how rarely help students learn.

( )( )( )( )( )46. Letting students determine learning objectives wastes too much time in irrelevant discussion.

( )( )( )( )( )47. The primary concern of a teacher should be the immediate needs of the student.

( )( )( )( )( )48. Grades should reflect a students' grasp of the subject or skill taught.

SA   A   U   D   SD

( )( )( )( )( )49. Assignments by a teacher tend to restrict students' significant learnings.

( )( )( )( )( )50. Tests prepared by students are usually just as effective as those prepared by a teacher.

( )( )( )( )( )51. The goals a student sets for himself are the basis of effective learning not the teachers goals.

( )( )( )( )( )52. A teacher's mission is to help each student learn what he decides will aid him in achieving his personal goals.

( )( )( )( )( )53. If a teacher isn't careful, students take advantage.

SA   A   U   D   SD

( )( )( )( )( )54. Considering the possible effects on students, a teacher should usually play it safe rather than take chances.

( )( )( )( )( )55. Without a cooperative climate encouraging students to risk and experiment, significant learning is unlikely.

( )( )( )( )( )56. A teacher who does not plan the work for a class carefully is taking advantage of the students' ignorance.

( )( )( )( )( )57. To use students' experiences and resources for learning requires group activities rather than such methods as lectures..

( )( )( )( ) (58. It is a good rule in teaching to keep relationships with
) students impersonal.

SA   A   U   D   SD

( )( )( )( )( ) 59. Planning units of work should be done by students and teacher together.

( )( )( )( )( ) 60. Good teaching is systematic – set up a clear plan and schedule and stick to it.

Educational Orientation Questionnaire (EOQ)

Scoring Sheet

PEDAGOGICAL ITEMS	ANDROGOGICAL ITEMS	STANDARDIZED TOTAL SCORE
SA = 1, A = 2, U = 3, D = 4, SD = 5	SA = 5, A = 4, U = 3, D = 2, SD = 1	Total Raw Score = _____

PEDAGOGICAL	ANDROGOGICAL	
1. _____	2. _____	Subtract *210.8*
3. _____	4. _____	
5. _____	6. _____	Algebraic (+ or –) Remainder _____
7. _____	8. _____	
9. _____	10. _____	Divide Algebraic Remainder by 26 (or more
11. _____	12. _____	accurately by 25.924)
13. _____	14. _____	
15. _____	18. _____	_____ ÷26 (or 25.924)
16. _____	22. _____	Algebraic
17. _____	24. _____	Remainder
19. _____	25. _____	
20. _____	26. _____	= _____ Standardized Score
21. _____	28. _____	
23. _____	30. _____	Percent of Adult Educators with EOQ Scores
27. _____	31. _____	Less than or Greater than Your Score
29. _____	33. _____	(Standardized)
32. _____	35. _____	

Your Score	% of Scores Less	Your Score	% of Scores
Greater			
-1.0	15.87	+1.0	15.87
-1.5	6.68	+1.5	6.68
-2.0	2.28	+2.0	2.28
-2.5	0.62	+2.5	0.62
-3.0	0.13	+3.0	0.13

34. _____	36. _____
37. _____	38. _____
39. _____	40. _____
41. _____	43. _____
42. _____	45. _____
44. _____	47. _____
46. _____	49. _____
48. _____	50. _____
53. _____	51. _____
54. _____	52. _____
56. _____	55. _____
58. _____	57. _____
60. _____	59. _____
TOT _____	+ _____

For example: If your standardized score is +1.5, then, in the theoretical population of all adult educators, 6.68 percent will have a score more andragogically oriented (Larger) than yours or, alternatively, 93.32 percent will have a score more pedagogically oriented (Less) than yours.

= _____ Total Raw Score

LESSON PLAN

Goal

To translate the concept of educational philosophy into concrete teaching behaviors.

Objectives:

To define educational philosophy.
To discern how teaching behaviors relate to philosophy.
To contrast teaching and learning in the educational process.

Pre-Opening

Ask each participant to formulate a metaphor to describe his or her teaching. Share some examples.

I. Introduction

Philosophy is an abstract concept. Defining what it is in terms of how teaching behaviors reflect philosophy makes it concrete and visible. Why is it important to answer the question, "Why teach?" Ask a few from group to share their response to, "Why teach?"

II. Body

What is the purpose of teaching? Discuss.
Reflect on teaching philosophy and write a statement of what your philosophy is?
What are the three domains of learning and give examples of each.
Complete the Zinn Philosophy of Adult Education Inventory and Hadley's Educational Orientation Questionnaire. Discuss the implications of the results.

III. Conclusion

Ask participants to share their personal philosophy. Indicate what process they intend to use to regularly examine and evaluate their philosophy.
Resources: Various philosophy instruments.

WORKSHEET

What is the purpose of teaching?

Why do you teach?

What are the rewards of teaching for you?

What frustrates you most about teaching?

Write a metaphor to describe your teaching.

What is your personal philosophy of teaching?

Complete PAEI© Inventory. What do the results indicate?

Complete the Educational Orientation Questionnaire. What do the results indicate about your teaching?

What process will you use to continually examine and evaluate your philosophy?

What theory of learning most closely parallels your own beliefs?

What are the three domains of learning? Provide examples of each.

Chapter 3

STYLES

"Whoever cares to learn will always find a teacher."

- German Proverb

TEACHING STYLES

Style =
a) a distinctive or characteristic manner
b) a method of acting or performing, especially as sanctioned by some standard
c) overall excellence, skill or grace in performance or manner.

Teaching style describes the behaviors, methods, and the communication process used to transmit information. Teaching style encompasses those qualities that are consistent in all situations and in all content areas.

Style refers to the overt means by which teachers convey their attitudes (philosophy) about the teaching/learning transaction. Teachers do have definite opinions about teaching methods and these relate strongly to their classroom practice.

Teaching style makes a significant difference in student achievement. Teachers must use a style that treats adults with dignity and respect. Any teaching approach needs to reflect trust and a sense that the teacher is available to help students learn.

Common styles include:

Authoritarian - teacher believes it is his/her job to fill the empty container the student brings to him/her.

Socratic - teacher asks a series of questions, each designed to draw students gradually to their own awareness of the issue - believes students have all the answers in their heads, but need expert guidance to draw out the answers.

Heuristic - teacher believes in trial and error and learning from experience.

Collaborative - teacher allows students to explore, discuss and negotiate together.

Counseling - teacher draws on the affective, utilizes theories of Carl Rogers suggesting a non-directive style, using reflective questions with learning proceeding based on the students' discovery and curiosity.

Facilitative - teacher serves as a guide. This style comes from the Latin word "facil" to make easy.

There are four major categories of styles which are explained in Chapter 7. Briefly introduced here, they are:

Style		*Method*
instructor-centered	=	lecture
interactive	=	questions, discussion, debate
individual	=	reading, projects, computers
experiential	=	field trips, labs, hands-on exercises

Figure 3: Teaching Style

Why Identify Teaching Style?

1. to improve your delivery to students
2. to make decisions for future teaching sessions
3. to assist in planning for faculty development
4. to help you understand your classroom behavior
5. to match with the styles of your learners
6. to make decisions related to the learning environment.
7. to state beliefs about teaching
8. to identify role as a teacher

Your style developed over time, from your personality (most teachers are extroverts), from recollections of the way you were taught (teachers model the way they were taught), and from training undertaken to improve skills. Your experiential background influenced your style as well because your style matches your own learning style. Teachers begin to use a more collaborative style as both their age and their training increases.

Conti (1990) developed the Principles of Adult Learning Scale to help teachers identify their style. It is available at the end of the chapter on page . In addition to using it for personal assessment, it can be freely used for other purposes including research.

Changing   Styles

1. Student demographics have changed dramatically. Students today look much different than a description of a college student 30 years ago who was predominately white, male, and 18 years old. For example, there is an influx of older students who express a need for education to be an "active experience." Some reasons for this shift over recent years are:

   the reentry of women in the 1960s
   the influx of students over 25 years from 1970-85
   the decrease of students under 25. By the mid 80s, 50% of students were over 25 years, and that trend continues in the 90s.

2. Different styles are used appropriately to match with teaching goals
3. More training

4. More experience
5. To appeal to more students' learning styles

Problems in Changing Style

-   learners have been socialized to believe education is authoritarian and expect to be taught by an "authority"
-   teachers who want power and control and have a need to dominate
-   standardized curriculum which can limit your flexibility
-   economics
-   lack of training
-   learners who strongly want a teacher-centered experience
-   no one way to teach has been identified as the best
-   mix of students in class
-   hard work to change and style changes slowly
-   risky
-   ego involvement
-   motivation

My advice is to use a variety of methods and materials so you can be versatile based on the mix of students and the learning goals.

Both the substantive and stylistic levels of teaching are needed to capture the attention of the group.

LEARNING STYLES

When teachers understand how students learn, they can develop insights into how to design instruction that responds to individual learning needs. What follows can assist teachers to identify types of learning styles, and to discover strategies to integrate teaching style with learning style.

Learning style is defined as the way in which an individual approaches a learning situation to perceive and process information. Style tends to be eclectic, but most learners have a dominate style that emerges. Learning style is also described as how a learner collects, organizes and transforms information into useful knowledge (Cross, 1981). Style reflects behaviors that indicate how a person learns from his or her environment or in response to particular situations.

A learning preference is how one best likes to learn and, therefore, prefers this mode if given a choice. Learning strategies are those tactics used by students to adapt to whatever situation they are confronted with. So, they are able to learn effectively.

Strategies may actually be more important than learning style for successful learning. Despite learners' preferences for conditions, contents, and modes of learning, students seem to devise ways to successfully learn by determining what the teacher wants. Here is how one student adapted:

"I figured it out in the third grade when I turned in my book report early. I did it early because I really loved the book. The teacher was ecstatic! I figured I'd do that again."

- Oprah Winfrey, July 7, 1995

Learning efficiency may be fostered by making students aware of their styles and by providing counseling for them on how to adapt their styles to the course content. There are also strategies for strengthening their less developed learning style areas.

Learning style can be subdivided into three areas:- information gathering and receiving (visual, auditory, tactile)- social conditions (work in groups or alone)- expressiveness (written or verbal reporting)

Why Discover Learning Styles?

1. no one style works for everyone; each student has a unique style
2. to recognize and accommodate the style that fits best
3. to strengthen weak channels
4. to match with teaching style
5. some learning styles are more appropriate for certain content or learning situations
6. to expand learning capacity and enhance student's learning efficiency
7. to help learner be successful as measured by achievement
8. to facilitate learning
9. to predict some careers

How To Identify Learning Styles

Educators Rita and Ken Dunn tell the story of three children who each received a bicycle for Christmas. The bikes, purchased unassembled had to be put together by the parents. Tim's father read the directions carefully before he set to work. Mary's father laid out the pieces on the floor and handed the instructions to Mary's mother. "Read this to me," he said, as he surveyed the components. George's mother instinctively began fitting pieces together, glancing at the directions only when stymied. By evenings end, all three bikes were assembled, each using a different approach. The parents had worked according to their own learning styles: visual, auditory, and tactile.

Visual = students learn best by seeing words and pictures. They tend to take notes on what they hear because they remember best what they see. As part of their recall, they are able to close their eyes and visualize statements from a textbook. They have difficulty remembering a telephone number recited to them verbally.

Auditory = students learn from hearing words spoken or explanations made verbally. They may read aloud, especially when encountering new material.

Tactile (Kinesthetic or Haptic) = students learn best through the experiences that allow them to touch and feel. They are stimulated by the manipulation of objects. Touching, handling, and doing are important to their learning.

Some subjects or content areas are best learned by certain styles.

Auditory = music, languages

Tactile = typing, piano, computers, labs

Visual = abstract concepts such as physics, chemistry, and terminology associated with content.

Another simple way is for students to reflect about situations in which they find it easiest and most pleasant to learn. They can complete various instruments that will assist them in determining their learning styles. Refer to selected instruments included at end of this chapter.

Student's learning style is also dependent on the setting. The Dunns have developed a Productivity Environment Preference Survey, which identifies 21 elements that affect the way people learn. The 21 factors consider such items as noise level, lighting, and time of day.

Some students learn best working in groups and others when working independently where outcomes are based on individual merit. In measuring outcomes, some students do better in written reports, or tests, and some excel at expressing their learning orally. These students talk fluently, and are comfortable in articulating what they mean.

Learning style is evident in work methods. Do you prefer composing memos and letters at the computer, or talking into a dictaphone? The former suggests a visual preference, and the later leans toward an auditory style.

Student learning is influenced by a tendency to have a dominate left brain or a dominate right brain. Some traits of left brain learners are that they perceive analytically, hold an impersonal orientation, are able to structure situations, and are interested in new concepts for their own sake. Right brain learners perceive globally, look for relationships, like social situations, like material to be relevant, and want organization and structure provided.

Likewise, certain teaching traits are associated with left brain or right brain tendencies. Left brain teachers like to lecture, are strong in organizing, provide corrective feedback, and are teacher-centered in their approach. Right brain teachers prefer teaching formats that encourage interaction and discussion, strong in establishing a supportive environment, provide little feedback, and are student-centered.

Learning by using all three styles is rewarding because we retain:

> 25% of what we hear
> 45% of what we hear and see
> 70% of what we hear, see, and do
> (Sandy, 1990, p. 80)

Factors that affect learning style include:

1. personality
2. subject matter or content
3. environment
4. perceived interest or relevancy or own motivation
5. teacher's style*
6. form of assessment used

*Student style seems to be impacted the most by the teaching style and by the form of assessment that is used.

Types of Learning Styles

Agnes G. Rezler's Learning Preference Inventory (1981) is an instrument that gives you the chance to indicate those conditions or situations which most facilitate your learning. The Inventory determines learning preference in six areas. The six areas are:

Abstract - preference for learning theories and generating hypotheses, with focus on general principles and concepts.

Concrete - preference for learning tangible, specific, practical tasks with the focus on skills.

Teacher-structured - preference for learning in a well-organized teacher-directed class, with expectations, assignments, and goals clearly identified by the teacher.

Student-structured - preference for learning via student-organized tasks, with emphasis on autonomy and self-direction.

Individual - preference for learning or working alone, emphasis on self-reliance and solitary tasks such as reading.

Interpersonal - preference for learning or working with others in group situations, with emphasis on harmonious relationships between students and teacher and among students.

The scoring shows a higher score in each of the three sets. A learning preference is revealed indicating a choice of the type of material (abstract or concrete), the way the material is delivered (teacher or student), and the social conditions under which the learning takes place (groups or one person).

David A. Kolb identifies a model of learning as a four-stage cycle. Effective learners need ability in four different areas: they must be able to involve themselves fully, openly, and without bias in new experiences (Concrete Experience, CE); to view these experiences from many perspectives (Reflective Observation, RO); to create concepts that integrate their observations into logically sound theories (Abstract Conceptualization, AC); and to use these theories to make decisions and solve problems (Active Experimentation, AE).

Kolb's Learning-Style Inventory (LSI, revised 1985) consists of 12 sentences about the way people learn and deal with ideas and day-to-day situations in life. Respondents read the sentences, and then rank-order the four endings provided from how they learn best to how they learn least. Scoring indicates if they learn best in a feeling, watching, thinking or doing mode. For example:

I learn best when:

   4 I trust my hunches and feelings   *2* I listen and watch carefully

1 I rely on logical thinking   *3* I work hard to get things done

This instrument is easy to use to help assess learning style. It takes about ten minutes to complete and is self-scored. The results have also shown valid relationships between learning style and career field choices. The LSI can be purchased from McBer and Company, 116 Huntington Avenue, Boston, MA 02116. Call 1-800-729-8074 for information.

Grasha and Riechmann's Learning Styles Questionnaire (1972) reveals six learning styles by categorizing student answers to 36 questions. The categories that describe learners are:

Competitive
Collaborative
Independent
Participant
Dependent
Avoidance

This instrument is located at the end of this section on page 59.

Locating hidden figures is a test to help students determine if they learn by being more "field dependent" or "field independent."

Barbe Modality Checklist is designed to provide a key to students' learning strengths based on if students use the visual, auditory, or tactile modality for learning. This instrument consists of 10 incomplete sentences, each followed by three ways of completing the sentence. The instrument is reprinted on page 63 at the end of this chapter.

How Styles Develop and Change

Here are some ideas to strengthen students' weaker learning channels and enhance their learning styles.

Consider this example. Imagine yourself as a student who purchased a computer and you want to learn to use it. If you are a visual learner, you will probably read the manual or watch someone demonstrate the use of the computer while you observe.

If you are an auditory learner, you may need to listen to someone explain the directions to you or you read them aloud. You would benefit from a lecture on using computers.

As a tactile learner, you will want hands-on experience right from the start.

The visual learner has the edge in school because reading is a visual activity. But the visual learner may have difficulty later if he or she does not develop good listening and communication skills as well.

Listening to someone tell a story is one way to improve listening skills, especially if you take time to talk about specific details in the story afterwards.

Young students can improve listening skills by playing a simple game of "I went on a picnic". Begin the game with the first student saying, "I went on a picnic and I took apples." The next student repeats that line and add a new picnic ingredient that starts with the next letter of the alphabet. For example, bananas.

Visual learners can develop auditory skills with the following exercise. Students stand blindfolded at a blackboard, and draw a picture using only the oral instructions provided by the teacher.

To help visual learners, encourage them to think in "pictures," and use a vivid imagination. While the teacher speaks, they can make the words into pictures by writing lists, drawing symbols and diagrams. It is easier for students to retain the spoken message if they develop a content outline, not only the teacher's words, but also their textbooks and class notes. It is helpful to organize notes into meaningful units or study charts. These visual learners really appreciate highlight markers.

Auditory learners work best when they hear new information. These students paraphrase directions and ideas, talk through problems, and accomplish new activities by talking about what to do and how to do it. A tape recorder is a terrific ally for efficient studying. After a lecture, these students can summarize the lecture on a tape and play it back for review, rather than relying on printed notes. They benefit by stating words aloud when reading. Even more useful, they can read into a tape recorder and use it to review on their way to school.

To strengthen this learner, an exercise to improve visual recall can be used. Place a variety of interesting objects on a tray. Allow the learner to study them for 30-45 seconds. Take the tray away and ask the student to write a list containing as many of the items as are remembered.

Another activity is to provide the student with a design on a paper. The complexity of the design can be simple, such as a basket of three different kinds of fruit, or a more abstract design consisting of a collection of geometric figures where the squares, triangles, and circles do not represent a concrete figure. The student looks at the design for two minutes, then places it face down and attempts to recreate the design. After this first round, students are given 30 seconds to view the design again and make modifications.

Tactile learners need to touch items, hold items, and move around while learning. Unless the tactile learners are fortunate to have teachers who espouse and practice active learning, these students can be at a disadvantage. They like to keep their hands busy by writing on the chalkboard, gesturing with their hands and arms, and often they create or build objects that represent concepts to help them remember. Reading aloud will help develop skills. These students can increase their ability to follow instructions by practicing a series of oral directions.

Six Keys to Learning

1. Look at the big picture first. You can increase your comprehension and retention if you scan the material first. Skim the subheadings, photo captions, and any available summaries.
2. Slow down and talk out loud. This is effective for absorbing complex and challenging work.
3. Practice Mnemonics to aid your memory. To name the five Great Lakes, use "HOMES" (Huron, Ontario, Michigan, Erie, and Superior). To name the planet system in order, "My very educated mother just served us nine peaches." (Mercury, Venus, Earth, Mars, Jupiter, Saturn, Uranus, Neptune, and Pluto.) Five types of memory can be remembered with the mnemonic WIRES--working, implicit, remote, episodic, and semantic.
4. Organize facts into categories. To remember all former U.S. Presidents in order, cluster them into groups: before the War of 1812, 1812-Civil War, Civil War-World War I, and those after WWI.
5. Focus your attention. Ask yourself when reading, "What do I want to learn from this, and how will I benefit from the knowledge gained?"
6. Whichever style you prefer and works best for you, remember you can expand your learning capacity and this can make your learning more productive.

This chapter provided ways for teachers to develop insights into their styles and devise strategies for integrating teaching styles with learning styles. A range is desirable. Teaching is like listening to a radio; some prefer country music, some jazz, and some revel in golden oldies.

"I am not a teacher, only a fellow traveller of whom you asked the way. I pointed ahead-ahead of myself as well as you."

- George Bernard Shaw

LEARNING STYLE QUIZ

Circle the number by the statements that accurately describe your behavior. For each statement, find the corresponding number below. A number of statements in one category is an indication of your learning style.

1. I am quiet; I rarely volunteer answers.
2. I love to communicate. I talk a lot!
3. I relate to people more in body and actions than using words.
4. I love putting together a difficult puzzle.
5. I am in perpetual motion. I do not like to sit still.
6. I remember jingles and television commercials.
7. I look neat and being well dressed is important to me.
8. I try to touch most things I see.
9. I am especially observant of details.
10. I have an untidy appearance and my room and desk are messy.
11. I am distracted rather easily by background noises.
12. I have a vivid imagination.
13. I stomp my feet and slam the door when I get angry.
14. In my spare time, I like to watch TV or see a movie.
15. I am very verbal and can easily express my feelings.
16. In my spare time, I enjoy listening to the radio, tapes or CDs.
17. I prefer to try things out by touching and feeling.
18. I get upset, but I hold in my feelings.
19. I prefer to do physical things in my spare time like golf, swimming, running, or tennis.
20. I can assemble almost anything without printed instructions.
21. I sort out problems by talking about them with others.
22. I naturally sound out words and I am a good speller.
23. I find it hard to pay attention when someone reads aloud.
24. I hear oral directions well and can follow them easily.

Answers:
VISUAL: 1, 4, 7, 9, 12, 14, 18, 23
AUDITORY: 2, 6, 11, 15, 16, 21, 22, 24
KINESTHETIC: 3, 5, 8, 10, 13, 17, 19, 20

LEARNING STYLE QUIZ

Place a check beside the statements that seem true of you. Then look below to determine if you are predominately a visual, auditory, or tactile learner.

1. ____I learn best by reading on my own.
2. ____I learn a lot by listening to lectures.
3. ____I enjoy classes that have physical activity involved.
4. ____I am able to learn how to do something by watching a demonstration.
5. ____I find class discussions are helpful to me.
6. ____I like to type and use computers.
7. ____Charts, diagrams and illustrations improve my understanding of topics.
8. ____When an instructor explains something, I learn more than when I read the information.
9. ____I get more out of labs and experiments than lecture classes because of the hands-on approach.
10. ____I find how-to manuals and printed directions helpful.
11. ____I like to use cassette tapes.
12. ____I prefer to work with machines and equipment rather than just listening to or reading explanations.
13. ____I can do anything if I am shown how by someone.
14. ____I can follow directions best when they are read aloud to me.
15. ____It is not enough to have someone show me, I have to do it myself.

Answers:
VISUAL: 1, 4, 7, 10, 13
AUDITORY: 2, 5, 8, 11, 14
TACTILE: 3, 6, 9, 12, 15

STUDENT LEARNING STYLES QUESTIONNAIRE: GENERAL FORM

The following questionnaire has been designed to help you clarify your attitudes and feelings toward the courses you have taken in college and to identify your preferred learning style(s). Remember, formulate your answers with regard to your general attitudes and feelings toward your courses.

Write your answers on the space provided by each question. Write the number that best explains how you feel about the statement as follows:

Mark 1 if you strongly disagree with the statement.
Mark 2 if you moderately disagree with the statement.
Mark 3 if you are undecided.
Mark 4 if you moderately agree with the statement.
Mark 5 if you strongly agree with the statement.

==

1.____Most of what I know, I learned on my own.
2.____I have a difficult time paying attention during class sessions.
3.____I find the ideas of other students relatively useful for helping me to understand the course material.
4.____I think a teacher who lets students do whatever they want is not doing his/her job well.
5.____I like other students to know when I have done a good job.
6.____I try to participate as much as I can in all aspects of a course.
7.____I study what is important to me and not necessarily what the instructor says is important.
8.____I feel that I have to attend class rather than feeling that I want to attend.
9.____I think an important part of classes is to learn to get along with other people.
10.____I accept the structure a teacher sets for a course.
11.____To get ahead in class, I think sometimes you have to step on the toes of the other students.
12.____I do not have trouble paying attention in classes.
13.____I think I can determine what the important content issues are in a course.
14.____If I do not understand course material, I just forget about it.

15.____I think students can learn more by sharing their ideas than by keeping their ideas to themselves.
16.____I think teachers should clearly state what they expect from students.
17.____I think students have to be aggressive to do well in school.
18.____I get more out of going to class than staying at home.
19.____I feel that my ideas about content are often as good as those in a textbook.
20.____I try to spend as little time as possible on a course outside of class.
21.____I like to study for tests with other students.
22.____I like tests taken right out of the book.
23.____I feel that I must compete with the other students to get a grade.
24.____I attend classes because I want to learn something.
25.____I am confident in my abilities to learn important course material.
26.____School does not really interest me.
27.____I think students should be encouraged to work together.
28.____I feel that facts presented in textbooks and lectures are correct.
29.____I like the teacher to notice me.
30.____I feel that classroom activities are generally interesting.
31.____I like to think things through for myself before a teacher lectures on course material.
32.____I seldom get excited about material covered in a course.
33.____I prefer not to work alone on assignments.
34.____Before working on a class project, I try to get the approval of the instructor.
35.____To do well in a course, I have to compete with the other students for the teacher's attention.
36.____I do my assignments before reading other things that interest me.

SCORE SHEET

Transfer the number 1-5 you indicated on the line next to number of the statement. Total each column. The highest number is indicative of your dominate learning style.

INDEPENDENT	AVOIDANCE	COLLABORATIVE
1____	2____	3____
7____	8____	9____
13____	14____	15____
19____	20____	21____
25____	26____	27____
31____	32____	33____
Total ____	Total ____	Total ____

DEPENDENT	COMPETITIVE	PARTICIPANT
4____	5____	6____
10____	11____	12____
16____	17____	18____
22____	23____	24____
28____	29____	30____
34____	35____	36____
Total ____	Total ____	Total ____

Grasha and Riechmann (1972). Used with permission.

Student Learning Styles Identified by Anthony Grasha and Sheryl Riechmann

Competitive. This response style is exhibited by students who learn material in order to perform better than others in the class. They feel they must compete with other students in the class for the rewards of the classroom, such as grades or teachers' attention. They view the classroom as a win-lose situation, in which they must always win.

These learners prefer to be the group leader in discussions or when working on projects. They ask questions in class and like to be singled out for doing a good job. They have no real preference for any teaching method other than a slightly more teacher-centered focus than student-centered.

Collaborative. This style is typical of students who feel they can learn the most by sharing ideas and talents. They cooperate with teachers and peers and like to work with others. They see the classroom as a place for social interaction as well as content learning.

Learner prefers lectures with class discussion in small groups, and group projects rather than individual. Prefers student-designed courses and peer determined grades.

Avoidance. This response style is typical of students who are not interested in learning course content in the traditional classroom. They do not participate with students and teachers in the classroom. They are uninterested or overwhelmed by what goes on in classes.

This learner is turned off by classroom activities, tests, and required reading and assignments. Prefers a blanket grade where everyone gets a passing grade.

Participant. This style is characteristic of students who want to learn course content and like to go to class. They take responsibility for getting the most out of class and participate with others when told to do so. They feel that they should take part in as much of the class related activity as possible and little that is not part of the course outline.

These students like opportunities to discuss material. They also like both objective and essay type tests. Prefer an enthusiastic teacher who can analyze and synthesize material well.

Dependent. This style is characteristic of students who show little intellectual curiosity and who learn only what is required. They see teacher and peers as sources of structure and support. They look to authority figures for guidelines and want to be told what to do.

These students need a teacher prepared outline and written notes on the board. They want clear deadlines for assignments and definitely desire teacher-centered methods.

Independent. This response style is characteristic of students who like to think for themselves. They prefer to work on their own, but will listen to the ideas of others in the classroom. They learn the content they feel is important and are confident in their learning abilities.

These students excel at independent, self-paced study. They like to design their own projects and activities. They prefer a student-centered classroom.

Grasha and Riechmann 1972. Modified and used with permission.

FIND YOUR MODALITY STRENGTHS

Listed below are ten incomplete sentences and three ways of completing each sentence. Check the statement that is most typical of you. Then count the number of checks in each column. This will give you a rough idea of the relative strength of each of your modalities.

1. My emotions can often be interpreted from my: ( ) Facial expressions   ( ) Voice quality   ( ) General body tone

2. I keep up with current events by: ( ) Reading the newspaper thoroughly when I have time   ( ) Listening to the radio or watching the television news   ( ) Quickly reading the paper or spending a few minutes watching television news

3. If I have business to conduct with another person, I prefer: ( ) Face-to-face meetings or writing letters   ( ) The telephone, since it saves time   ( ) Conversing while walking, jogging, or doing something else physical

4. When I'm angry, I usually: ( ) Clam up and give others the "silent treatment"   ( ) Am quick to let others know why I'm angry   ( ) Clench my fists, grasp something tightly, or storm off

5. When driving I; ( ) Frequently check the rear view mirrors and watch the road carefully   ( ) Turn on the radio as soon as I enter the car   ( ) Can't get comfortable in the seat and continually shift position

6. I consider myself: ( ) a neat dresser   ( ) a sensible dresser   ( ) a comfortable dresser

7. At a meeting I: ( ) come prepared with notes and displays   ( ) enjoy discussing issues and hearing other points of view   ( ) would rather be somewhere else and so spend my time doodling

8. In my spare time I would rather:	( ) watch television, go to a movie, and attend the theatre, or read	( ) listen to the radio or records, attend a concert, or play an instrument	( ) engage in a physical activity of some kind
9. The best approach to discipline is to:	( ) isolate the child by separating him or her from the group	( ) reason with the child and discuss the situation	( ) use acceptable forms of corporal punishment
10. The most effective way of rewarding students is through:	( ) positive comments written on their papers, stick-ons, or posting good work for others to see	( ) oral praise to the student and to the rest of the class	( ) a pat on the back, a hug, or some other appropriate physical action
Total number of boxes checked	___	___	___

LESSON PLAN

Goal - To discover what categories of teaching styles are available.

Objectives:
To identify types of teaching styles.
To determine your teaching style.
To select appropriate teaching style to fit situation.

Pre-Opening:

Show Teaching Style cartoon on overhead projector.

I. Introduction
Who can define teaching style?

What are the common teaching styles used?

Have respondent provide an actual demonstration of the style as a way of defining it.

II. Body
Why identify your teaching style?

How did your style develop?

Should style ever change?

How can your style be changed?

What problems might result in changing your style?

Complete the PALS instrument to determine if your teaching style is more teacher-centered or student-centered.

Ask for volunteers to share their results.

Conti's PALS instrument score Mean 146. The lower the score, the more teacher-centered you are, and the higher the score, the more learner-centered your style is.

III. Conclusion

Resources: Teaching Style Instrument, Cartoon

LESSON PLAN

Goal - To assist teachers in understanding how students learn and to develop instructional skills that respond to students' different learning styles.

Objectives:
To identify types of learning styles.
To recognize strategies that integrate teaching style with learning styles.

Pre-Opening:
Tell the Christmas story of three children's bicycles. As they listen to the story, ask participants to determine which method they would use.

I. Introduction
Define Learning Style, Learning Preference, and Learning Strategy.
In this session you will receive information about these three topics. This will help you understand how students learn in different ways. You will know how to provide opportunities in your instruction that appeal to the various learners.

II. Body
Why identify learning styles? Participants will give reasons.
Review three major styles: visual, auditory, and tactile.
How do these styles develop?
Participants will complete a sampling of instruments to identify their own learning style. Discuss the results.
Discuss how instruments are designed to determine different kinds of styles.
What can be done to strengthen the less dominate styles?
What instructional techniques can you use to accommodate the different styles?

III. Conclusion
Resources: Learning Style Instruments

WORKSHEET

What is your dominate teaching style?

How is your teaching style related to your learning style?

What kind of car resembles your teaching style?

What problems might you have in developing other styles?

Complete the PALS instrument.

What are the results of the various learning style instruments?

What kinds of students are in your classroom or sessions?

What specific ideas can you implement to appeal to as many different student learning styles as possible?

Chapter 4

LEARNING THEORIES AND ADULT LEARNING PRINCIPLES

"Education is what remains after one forgets everything he learned in school."

- Einstein

To address teaching without learning is like getting a kiss without a squeeze. The last three decades have seen scholars look at how adults learn to determine if their learning is different from how children learn. Malcolm Knowles' term "andragogy" emerged out of this pursuit. He defines andragogy as the "art and science of helping adults learn." Its counter term, pedagogy, the science of how children learn is derived from pedagogue, a Greek servant responsible for walking the master's children to school.

Agreement exists that the major theories do not differ drastically between how children and adults learn. Certain principles of adult learning have developed that deserve recognition. Awareness of these principles helps you as you approach teaching and determine the impact you have on the learning process.

Theory represents a set of plausible ideas that present a systematic view of a subject and is offered to explain phenomena.

Developing learning theory is a process of systematically accumulating a set of ideas or principles which stimulates thinking to explain the "why" behind the practice. Theory is helpful to gain insight into what you do as a teacher that impacts learning. A theory of adult learning enables you to understand how learning occurs, and as a teacher, helps you arrange for it to happen.

Three major learning theories are commonly recognized. Stimulus-response (S-R) conditioning behavior where the learner reacts by giving the desired response to appropriate stimuli. Conditioning is enhanced by reinforcing the desired behavior. The most common example of this type of learning is Pavlov's dogs who reacted to the sound of a bell by salivating even when no food was available. This behavior occurred because of the cues the dogs were conditioned to respond to in expectation of a reward.

Cognitive learning refers to individuals gaining new insights or knowledge. With this type of learning, individuals become storehouses of information. The key to cognitive learning is being able to retrieve the information whenever you need to access it. Developing a systematic way to organize information before it is entered into your brain is essential. This process parallels inputting data into a computer, and then finding it when you need it.

Mental discipline occurs when the mind is developed by exercising it, or simply using it. The analogy of athletes training their muscles can be useful in understanding how this method of learning occurs.

Learning principles are the underpinnings of learning theories. Understanding principles helps explain why certain strategies and techniques are more effective in the classroom than others. By incorporating learning principles into the classroom, students are afforded superior conditions of learning that foster their growth and development.

Here are principles I have gained from my experience and from other well known authors in the field of adult learning.

Adults have a wide reaching background of practical life experiences. These experiences contribute greatly to the direction and focus of their learning. They draw upon former knowledge to make connections with new information and to determine if it is compatible or in conflict with previously held ideas and values. Past experience makes a valuable contribution to collaborative learning situations where the variety and diversity of experiences can enrich the current learning by broadening each other's perspective.

Learning Principle - Build new learning by integrating it with past learning. Connect the unfamiliar to the familiar. Teaching is bridge building. Build bridges for students to walk across.

Adults generally enter a learning situation voluntarily and possess a variety of motivations.

1. Social Reasons - Learning fulfills a need for personal associations and friendships and develops a sense of belonging.
2. External Expectations - Most often these adults find themselves in learning situations at the recommendation of someone else. An example is when a supervisor instructs an employee to participate in training and development to increase competence in a job situation. Culture and religion also impose expectations.
3. Social Welfare - Adults attend educational programs to prepare them to understand community problems and to better serve the community by working toward solutions to the problems.
4. Professional Advancement - Adults have a strong desire to immediately apply what they have learned. This is accomplished in job situations and can lead to higher job status, increased skills that contribute to professional advancement, and new jobs.
5. Escape - Adults are motivated to seek education as a way to add variety to their routine life. Education is viewed as a means to relieve boredom and to introduce change in their existing lives.
6. Intellectual Development - Adults enjoy learning because they find it stimulating, and seem to learn wherever they are. Education satisfies and soothes an inquiring mind.
7. Personal Fulfillment - Adults discover that education makes them happier and they develop a stronger sense of well-being.

Learning Principle - Recognize motivation as a driving force that encourages adults to learn. This is an internal force that comes from the learner to promote action. Adults seek learning to achieve goals, for the activity provided, and/or for the sake of learning.

Adults develop habit patterns that are reinforced by stimuli and responses, so they tend to repeat those experiences where they receive positive responses. They function best with immediate feedback and positive reinforcement. Education meets a need for self-fulfillment.

Learning Principle - Recognize that adults base their self-concept on success or failure. They have a psychological need to develop a sense of well-being and to keep it intact. They are reluctant to take risks and attempt to minimize risk taking whenever possible. It is essential to develop mutual trust and respect.

Certain physiological changes occur in adults in the aging process. Visual acuity may decline. To compensate for this, adults can position themselves in the classroom where they can best see, often near the front where their view of the instructor and the chalkboard are unobstructed. Good lighting is tremendously helpful. Time constraints are counter-productive to learning and cause unnecessary stress. Allowing additional time for tasks and encouraging adults to set their own pace diminishes any negative impact on learning. Sitting for extended periods of time in uncomfortable chairs is also distracting. Frequent breaks, comfortable seating, and learning which provides opportunities to be physically active reduce these distractions.

Adults experiencing stress or anxiety can become stimulated in ways that cause them to resist learning. The goal in adult learning environments is to reduce barriers, eliminate threats, and convey friendliness and trust which are supportive to adult learning. Freedom of expression, mutual respect, and acceptance of differences also characterize a conducive learning environment.

Learning Principle - Provide a physically and psychologically comfortable environment for adult learning. Encourage learners to indicate what they need to learn successfully.

Adults frequently approach learning to assist them in problem-solving. They experience a gap between their wants and their current or desired level of ability or skill necessary to solve a problem. The teacher and the students mutually explore what is needed. Those needs are taken into account when objectives are developed to close the gap. Learning experiences are designed and resources identified to ensure progress toward the goal.

Learning Principle - Provide adults with immediate opportunities to practice and apply new skills and knowledge. Ensure that the learning content is relevant so adults perceive it as a way of meeting their needs and deem it to be meaningful and important.

Adults seek education as a response to coping with life changing events. Losing a job or a desire to change careers is a trigger for additional education to develop new skills.

Learning Principle - Be aware of adult development stages and the demand for different skills as adults encounter the different stages. Recognize how education helps them make successful transitions.

Adults enter educational situations with certain expectations and will articulate them when given a chance. Students are capable of taking responsibility for their learning. Education has become a shared relationship between teacher and learner where objectives are mutually agreed on. Students participate in needs assessment, evaluation of outcomes, and can negotiate learning contracts with teachers.

Learning Principle - The educational model has shifted to a student-centered model by moving away from the more traditional teacher-centered model. Work together to incorporate expectations of both clarifying and negotiating as needed.

Adult students want to actively participate in all aspects of their learning situations. They are not satisfied to be passive recipients of knowledge. They find learning challenging when they participate both physically and mentally. They see learning enhanced by two-way communication, and lean away from an authoritarian teaching model.

Learning Principle - Adults possess a desire to become self-directed. By taking the initiative in designing learning experiences, diagnosing needs, locating resources, and evaluating learning outcomes, they are prepared to become lifelong learners. This skill equips them to continue learning to keep abreast of rapidly changing technology and the information explosion.

Focusing on how learning takes place in adults is a relatively new field. Good, sound theory takes years of study, and collecting and analyzing empirical data. Because of its status as a young discipline, adult learning theory data are incomplete. What is important at this time is to recognize what is known about adult learning and the development of learning principles, and seek to incorporate those into your teaching situations.

"The teacher can decide what to teach, but only the learner decides what to learn."

LESSON PLAN

Goal - To gain an understanding of how people learn and to recognize the principles underpinning the theories.

Objectives:
To capitalize on techniques that influence how adults learn.
To incorporate learning principles into the learning environment.

Pre-Opening:
Think of a snappy attention getter to introduce this topic.

I. Introduction
Today's discussion explores how people learn. Principles that underlie the learning theories are identified. This session offers you techniques to incorporate into learning situations to assist, rather than hinder adults as they learn.

II. Body
Discuss overall learning theories. Have participants provide examples.
Ask group to offer strategies to incorporate into their sessions to help adults learn.
Discuss principles from reading. What other principles can group offer?
I have a collection of vingettes from movies and television that depict many principles. I use this videotape to demonstrate teaching techniques and philosophies.

III. Conclusion

Review
Summary
Resources:

WORKSHEET

What principles can you incorporate into your teaching to help students learn?

Chapter 5

ACTIVE LEARNING

"Students are like wheelbarrows. They stand still unless pushed!"

Richard Weaver, Professor Of Speech
Bowling Green State University

Is learning a noun or a verb?

If learning is a noun, it is thought of as an item that is passed along in a neat package. Learning as a verb, indicates it is an action process with students thinking and doing. This chapter incorporates the concept of active learning and presents strategies that assist both teachers and learners in the educational process.

DEVELOPING CRITICAL THINKING

Active learning is any method or technique that gets students to do something other than sit passively in the classroom. Activity or action is the key to learning. Learning means a change takes place, and students change by doing, not by listening. To be active learners, students are engaged physically and mentally. They are doing things, and also thinking about what they are doing. This is the process of critical thinking.

This chapter is meant to develop the teacher's philosophical as well as technical skills to involve the students. Ways of encouraging students to become active participants in the learning process are included.

Helping identify and overcoming student barriers to become active learners will include how to provide response opportunities for students, define different levels of participation, and understand motivation.

To incorporate active learning in the classroom requires an attitude that there is less emphasis on transmitting information in a learning situation along with possessing the skills and techniques that promote participation. To promote active learning requires giving up some control.

King (1993) describes the professor as the central figure, the "sage on the stage," the one who has the knowledge and transmits that knowledge to the students, who simply memorize the information and later reproduce it on an exam, often without even thinking about it. Known as the transmittal model of teaching, it assumes that the student's brain is an empty container into which the professor pours knowledge. Students are passive. Such a view is outdated. Students need to know how to think, solve problems, and produce, rather than reproduce, knowledge. Knowledge is a state of understanding as well as application.

In the model of constructivist, the student is at the center of the process. The facilitator "guide on the side" presents the material in a way that causes the students to do something with the information - interact with it, manipulate the ideas, and relate them to what they already know.

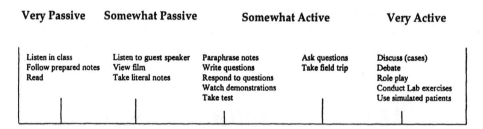

Figure 4.
Active learning continuum.

Advances in Chiropractic©, vol. 3
©1996, Mosby-Year Book, Inc.
Kay F. Quam
Problem-based Learning, 377-393

An active learning environment provides students a chance to talk and listen, read, write, and reflect using the higher order thinking skills of analysis, synthesis, and evaluation. When students talk and write, their thinking is clarified. When students reflect on information, they gain greater insight into the knowledge. When students read, their comprehension is increased when they are provided a guide or specific instructions, such as asking students to summarize the main points. They are actively engaged with the goal for learning to use and apply the information gained from the course. In so doing, they are able to retain the information by using it.

Students learn in different ways. To acknowledge this difference in learning styles and past experiences, active learning utilizes a wide variety of activities, and therefore appeals to a diverse student group.

One simple way of introducing active learning to students is to insert brief writing assignments in the classroom. For example, after 15-20 minutes spent covering content, pause and have students write down the main points covered.

Students can break into groups of three or four, and engage in a discussion after 20 minutes of course content has been presented. They can discuss ways of applying the content to real experiences. They can formulate questions they have and ask for clarification of ideas that are unclear to them.

An exercise that introduces physical activity and also facilitates critical thinking and values clarification can be conducted to reinforce course content. The four corners of the room are designated as: 1)Strongly Agree, 2) Agree, 3) Disagree, and 4) Strongly Disagree. A statement is read and students are asked to place themselves in the corner that most represents their opinions. For example, "Lectures should be outlawed." Students are randomly selected to justify their position. This exercise illustrates the diversity of opinions and affords participants an opportunity to develop communication skills. (Sloan & Wissmann, 1996).

Field trips provide a very active learning experience where students are transported to a real situation. Ask students to recall a memorable time from elementary school, and likely they will remember a meaningful field trip.

Simulations can offer a substitute if field trips are not logistically possible. Simulations are designed to approximate examples of real things. This allows students to experience similar situations while under supervision so adverse consequences are reduced.

Journals are a simple, yet powerful tool to allow students to reflect about what they are learning, and to write about their thinking and feelings. Journals provide important feedback to teachers. Concepts and ideas that students are unclear about can be documented. Students can note connections they make between classroom information and real life applications. Their writing combined with reflection increases students' understanding about issues.

Everyone acknowledges the possibilities and the potential for active learning created when computers were introduced in the classroom. The technology is beneficial at all levels of education. Limited technology was employed in the classroom over the years. The emphasis was placed on the human aspects such as relationships and a warm and supportive learning environment where trust and respect were practiced. Retain that emphasis as you introduce technology. It supports, but cannot substitute. Technology provides an extension of the teacher and frees up time to do more one-on-one teaching.

Science can be abstract, but when formulas and principles come to life in laboratory exercises, students see abstract concepts become visible and easier to comprehend.

Role play, discussed in Chapter 7, is another form of active learning. Students play out designated roles in dramatic ways that bring action to the classroom, both for the players and for the students observing.

Brainstorming, also discussed in Chapter 7, is a low cost, fast moving technique that allows students to be active learners in a low risk way by sharing ideas while suspending any form of evaluation.

Students who develop oral presentations are engaged in active learning. Researching topics, synthesizing and organizing information, and verbally presenting information is active learning.

OVERCOMING BARRIERS TO LEARNING

Active learning is a strong component of the newer model of education where students share responsibility with the teacher for the educational process. This involves change for both students and teachers. Students may have barriers that prevent them from being active.

Cynicism can be reduced when countered with a positive attitude and projecting a sense of optimism.

Undue criticism becomes a determent for learning when the learner takes few risks because of fear of failure. Criticism can be eliminated when everyone practices respect and values ideas. Fear of criticism affects self-confidence and ego.

Dominance is characteristic of the older model of education when the teacher is viewed as the authority. Teachers who do most of the talking can be seen as overpowering and dominating. By introducing students to shared responsibilities, dominance is eliminated.

Lack of interest by students can be overcome by making content and activities relevant. Opportunities to apply content to real life experiences is essential.

Risk can diminish the activity undertaken by students. If the learning environment is threatening, students are reluctant to participate in activities necessary for active learning. By gradually introducing students to one or two different techniques or exercises, risk can be reduced.

To reduce the risk barrier, add activities with a low risk level, and gradually increase to higher levels of risk. There is virtually no risk when students are passive during the showing of a film or listening to a lecture.

Low risk activities include small group discussions, brainstorming, in-class writing exercises, field trips, lectures with pauses, demonstrations, and responding to questionnaires.

Higher level risk activities are role play, oral presentation either individual or group, responding randomly to questions, and unstructured group discussions.

An environment with distractions causes competition for the message. Eliminating external interferences keeps the focus on learning.

When students feel psychologically and physically comfortable with no threat to their status and ego, they are eager to participate.

Instructors also have an element of risk when introducing active learning. Some fear that students may not react, participate, respond, or may deliberately sabotage situations. To alleviate this, recognize that some students do prefer passive learning, especially those who are auditory learners. Sometimes they resist because they have not been exposed to this method of learning. If introduced gradually, most students have a positive experience, and find they "like" this form of learning.

Teachers may fear that the additional time required for active learning will reduce the amount of course content they can cover. Of course, it is also important to teach students critical thinking and for them to develop a predisposition to learning. More and more, teachers are realizing that there is simply too much information and it is impossible to deliver everything you know to the students with the expectation they will learn it all. Some studies have found that students actually learn as much, or more when they are active because they are stimulated both physically and mentally and apply what they are learning.

Some teachers also fear the loss of control or power if students are allowed to share the responsibility for the teaching/learning process. Once they realize that everyone benefits, they can let go of this fear.

To overcome the fear of the risk involved, it is imperative for teachers to develop skills in motivating students, asking effective questions, and providing response opportunities and giving appropriate responses to student comments.

Approach the task of learning the following skills and refer to Chapter 10 on questioning techniques. The key to success is to practice these techniques.

RESPONSE OPPORTUNITIES

Response opportunities for students include:

1. answering questions
2. giving opinions (good technique because there are no right or wrong opinions)
3. speaking as a small group reporter
4. presenting a case
5. reacting to feedback

When students do respond, teachers need to give a positive response. There are different levels of responding.

1. Acknowledgement. There is no evaluation of the idea or information. The response given only indicates that the idea was heard.
2. Praise. The student is rewarded by hearing that the idea presented contains useful, good, or interesting information.
3. Restatement. This response indicates that the information is important because is being emphasized. Teacher can say, "So, what you are saying is..."
4. Probe. Here the teacher seeks more information by saying,"Tell me more."
5. Redirect. The teacher responds in a way that promotes interaction among students by asking another student to respond to or add to what the first student said. "Rob, what can you add to what Sue said?"

6. Action. When the teacher responds that the idea suggested will be implemented, this is further evidence that rewards and encourages participation.

LEVELS OF PARTICIPATION

There are three levels of participation for students.

1. When students are in a position where they are ready to learn, you have their attention. At this level, teachers have mastered the presentation skills outlined in this book. They create opportunities for students to respond. They vary the style to appeal to as much student diversity as possible. They hold students accountable for learning, they keep students alert and ready by telling them they will be active, and finally, they move around to hold their attention. Moving around the available space closes the distance so the learning climate becomes less sterile, more social, and more personal.

2. Once students are attentive, they are receptive. Their circuits are open and ready for the current to flow. The next skill is to build the level of student's interest by recipient engagement. To be engaged means to acknowledge the relationship of the class content to the student's needs. Teachers must strive to make the information relevant. They can enhance the situation by using stories, examples, comprehensive questions, and illustrations that accentuate the information. Students can experience emotions when put in make believe situations designed to evoke certain emotions. When students are interested, their motivation increases.

3. The third and highest level is to develop student involvement by having them determine objectives, plan the learning, make decisions, and evaluate the learning

MOTIVATION

Stimulation is separate from motivation. Student motivation comes from within. The steps are to involve the learner, arouse and maintain the appropriate frame of mind. One level leads to the next higher level. A skill is learned or a product created where there is indication that mental effort and physical energy has been expended.

The challenge for teachers in dealing with motivation can be approached as, "How to keep the music playing."

The sequence of motivation is:
Energy - Student has capacity to act.
Volition - Student makes choice to act.
Direction - Student determines purpose of action.
Involvement - Student continues to act.
Completion - Student finishes task or action.

Teachers deal with motivation by influencing student attitudes, detecting their needs, stimulating them through active learning, creating a change in affect, increasing their competence or skills towards mastery, and reinforcing students by making them aware of the positive results of their learning. This affirms them and allows their motivation to continue.

When planning any learning activity, or active learning exercise, ask yourself:

What will the students do?
What can I do to guarantee a positive attitude for this?
How does this activity meet the needs of the students?
What about this activity will stimulate the students?
What reinforcement does this activity provide, either
affectively or competence?

How do we know when active learning is working? Students demonstrate improved mastery over the content and they can apply the theories and concepts. Retention of information is greater, and the classroom is more lively. Attendance often increases, students ask more questions. And finally, the process feels more exciting to you.

In summary, learning is facilitated and knowledge is retained longer if the learner is actively involved, both in the process of acquiring and applying information. The role of the teacher is to facilitate. This is a departure from the traditional authoritarian model. Teachers are encouraged to use and to practice the teaching methods and techniques presented here as alternatives to the standard lecture. This allows for variety and appeals to students' different learning styles.

Students need to be comfortable enough in order to participate and be responsive. Mutual respect is essential for interaction to occur. The teacher helps diagnose the learner's current knowledge base, level of competence, readiness to learn, and degree of dependence, and makes every effort to move learners along the learning continuum from passive to active. This requires an atmosphere for learning that is supportive of the learners.

When learning to play the piano, the learner does not observe someone else play to learn the skill. The learner gets involved by putting his or her fingers on the keys and hears the music. They learn by doing, and the teacher helps by keeping the music playing.

> "I hear and I forget,
> I see and I remember,
> I do and I understand."
>
> - Confucius

LESSON PLAN

Goal - To develop teacher's skill in promoting active student learning as evidenced by learners' increased verbal participation.

Objectives:
To categorize levels of student participation.
To provide response opportunities for students.
To use responses that increase student participation.
To develop techniques to promote active learning.

Pre-Opening:
Ask the question, "Do you consider learning a noun or a verb? Ask for responses to include "why."

I. Introduction
Today we will:
This is important because:
At the end of the session, you will be able to:

II. Body
Ask participants to state what students do in class.

Have a volunteer list ideas on the blackboard. Develop an active learning continuum by having the responses given arranged from passive to active by the group. There may not be total agreement. Ask for rationale; then seek consensus. Example:

Students listen to lecture.   Conduct lab experiments.
Passive   Active

Responses could be written on poster board and held by respondents. Then ask others in group to arrange the people in a human continuum depicting a range from passive to active learning activities.

Discuss three levels of participation:

1. Get students' attention
2. Hold students' interest
3. Develop students' involvement

Brainstorm ways teacher can provide opportunities for students to respond i.e. become more active.

Example: give oral presentation

Have participants state some examples of typical responses they use when students respond.

Discuss six levels of responses. Choose six participants and give each a card with the level of response indicated. Make a comment, and ask a participant to respond using the level indicated on the card.

For example: You state, "I think groups function more effectively if they have a designated recorder." Now ask participant #1 to respond with a probe: "Tell me more." Participant #2 to respond with a restatement: "So, what you are saying is..."Participant #3 with a redirect: "Sue, what is your reaction to what Jim has stated?"

Discuss levels of risk for students to be more active. What barriers exist? Determine ways to reduce or eliminate risk.

Repeat the same exercise to identify risks for teachers.

What strategies have been used to appeal to students' motivation?

III. Conclusion

Review

Have each participant state one thing they currently do in the classroom that affords students the opportunity to be active.

In addition, what one thing did they learn as a result of this session that they plan to incorporate into the classroom to allow students to be more active learners?

Resources:

Index cards

Flip chart and markers

Poster Board

WORKSHEET

Passive _____ Active

Place an X on the line to indicate the type of learning that is typical of your teaching most of the time.

What can you do to help your students become critical thinkers?

What barriers exist in your teaching that prevent an active learning environment?

What response opportunities do students have in your sessions?

How can you "Keep the music playing?"

What can you do so students feel at ease and free to be responsive?

Chapter 6

CHARACTERISTICS OF GOOD TEACHING

"Information flows from the notes of the professor into the notebooks of the students, without passing through the minds of either!"

- K. Patricia Cross

This chapter is designed to assist faculty in identifying teacher characteristics that are effective in facilitating student learning. The goal is to develop an understanding of yourself. Included are techniques to assess teaching characteristics and to categorize those characteristics into three groups. Also presented are ways for improving teaching by developing those desirable characteristics.

Teaching is not easy. It is physically, emotionally, and intellectually demanding. How can you be a good teacher? Recognize that teaching is an art, a craft, and a profession. It involves not only knowledge of subject matter, but a talent for teaching, intelligence, a willingness to work hard at some drudgery like correcting exams and papers, and clarity of presentation. It takes exceptional people skills and a passionate commitment to learning about and promulgating knowledge of the subject matter being taught.

Teaching was one of the original four professions along with law, medicine, and theology. Originally held in high regard, reminders are sometimes necessary to dispel negative comments such as, "Those who can, DO, those who cannot, TEACH. Good teaching is necessary so students can learn, and also to uphold the prestige of the profession.

This is difficult because good teaching is hard to quantify. There are clear differences between what teachers and students consider good teaching. When faculty are asked what makes a good teacher, they emphasize intellectual traits and scholarly competence.

Students asked that same question are more concerned with personality. Students want faculty to stimulate them, to convey enthusiasm, to be organized, to encourage class discussion, and to relate the subject to the student's interest or application by providing lots of examples and illustrations.

Chickering and Gamson (1987) developed seven principles that help you achieve effectiveness.

1. good practice encourages student-faculty contact
2. good practice encourages cooperation among students
3. good practice encourages active learning
4. good practice gives prompt feedback
5. good practice emphasizes time on tasks
6. good practice communicates high expectations
7. good practice respects diverse talents and ways of learning

Brookfield (1986) stated "A great teacher has intensity and communicates it, not with a contrived act, but a genuine authentic presentation of the person." The person you seek to show has:

A genuine love for people.
An inquiring mind.
A curiosity for life beyond the classroom.
A professional attitude and a strong identity with the teaching profession.

These qualities prevent you from becoming a pedantic bore in your teaching.

Characteristics of good teaching that facilitate learning can be organized around three categories. A closer look at each category provides ideas to achieve excellence in each.

INTELLECTUAL (COGNITIVE AND PROFESSIONAL)

-   - ability to assess needs of students
-   - set realistic objectives
-   - develop content based on the objectives
-   - possess knowledge of subject
-   - understand theories of teaching and learning
-   - use evaluation often
-   - serve as a positive role model
-   - remain current and up-to-date
-   - display a genuine commitment to teaching
-   - demonstrate professional competence
-   - promote esprit de corp

PERSONAL

- make students feel comfortable
- use students' names frequently
- be a good listener
- be humanistically oriented
- demonstrate compassion and sensitivity
- display enthusiasm
- maintain a sense of humor
- foster a relationship with students
- be accessible to students
- strive to be open-minded, non-judgmental
- help build student's self confidence
- be genuinely interested in students
- exercise tolerance and patience
- respect individual uniqueness
- maintain your passion and dedication

INSTRUCTIONAL

-   - provide positive learning environment
-   - assess student needs
-   - prepare an organized plan

- - use appropriate teaching aids and materials
- - teach for comprehension
- - summarize major points
- - provide constructive feedback
- - use various teaching methods
- - be flexible, allow for the unexpected
- - involve students as partners
- - encourage questions
- - use appropriate gestures, maintain eye contact
- - vary voice tone, speed, and volume
- - provide opportunities for student success

Some Interesting Observations

"Teaching techniques don't teach, teachers do".

Being familiar with characteristics and qualities that define good teaching is beneficial. It is helpful to juxtapose those with student comments regarding what disappoints them the most about teachers.

Faculty who are not enthusiastic about their work or who look down on students.

Professors who promised to return papers by a certain date and then are perpetually late.

Professors who come in with graded papers and then tell you that grades aren't really important.

Here is how they responded to, "From your perspective, what is the most important thing faculty can do in the classroom to help students learn?"

They should challenge students more, instead of coddling them.

I'd advise professors to make it possible for students to ask questions and participate in class discussions.

Organization is very important, and some professors don't seem to have a game plan.

I'd advise some professors to learn something more about teaching. Sometimes professors who have a lot of knowledge do not

I'd advise some professors to learn something more about teaching. Sometimes professors who have a lot of knowledge do not communicate it because they lack some basic education keys or principles.
American Association for Higher Education (AAHE) Bulletin, 1993.)

Other pet peeves of students are:

1. Assign work as though their class is the only one, or at least the most important one.
2. Lecture too fast, and fail to slow down when requested.
3. Make students feel inferior when they ask a question.
4. Are not specific on what the test will cover.
5. Create "trick" questions.
6. Deliver their lecture in a monotone manner.
7. Give tests that don't correspond to lectures.
8. Get behind and then cram their lecture into the remaining time.
9. Assume students already have base knowledge for the course.
10. Require a textbook and then fail to use it.

(Ludewig, 1994)

Student behaviors that annoy teachers are listed in Chapter 16.

How To Improve and Do Better

1. Discover yourself. What is your style, how can you increase your versatility?
2. Discover the learners. What is their background, experience, and expectations? How can you appeal to their varied learning styles? How can you mesh?
3. Involve the learners by encouraging active participation. Consider opportunities for questions and student-centered activities and application of information and skills.
4. Vary your teaching techniques. Experiment with the multitude available and diversify. Increase your flexibility.
5. Ask for feedback from students and from colleagues. There is more about this endeavor in Chapter 15.
6. "Come prepared or don't come at all." (McDougle, 1981).

Self-Assessment

To assist you in determining your teaching strengths and identifying areas to strengthen, a series of assessment instruments is included. Some are general in nature, providing an overall assessment of teaching, and some are more specific for various teaching methods. This is intended as a positive experience to help you develop, grow, and learn.

"When you can't get a compliment any other way, pay yourself one."

- Mark Twain

SELF-ASSESSMENT QUESTIONNAIRES ON TEACHING

SELF-ASSESSMENT QUESTIONNAIRES

Two questionnaires are provided as a first step toward improving your lectures. The first asks that you rate yourself as a lecturer, group discussion leader, and tutor. In the second, you are asked to describe your feelings prior to, during, and after delivering a lecture.

Answer *all* questions. Following these questionnaires is a key for scoring your responses.

SELF-ASSESSMENT QUESTIONNAIRE (1)

Instructions (Please Read Carefully Before Beginning)

In this questionnaire you will see three sections headed by a phrase to be judged. Beneath it are pairs of contrasting words called scales which you are to use to rate the phrase. Make your judgments on the basis of what the phrase means to you. *This is not a test. There are no right or wrong answers.*

How to Use the Scales

The phrases to be judged appear in capital letters and the scales appear below them. Suppose you were to judge the phrase *my work* on the pair of words interesting-boring:

Interesting   7   6   5   4   3   2   1   Boring

First decide whether *my work* is interesting or boring; then decide *how* interesting or boring *you feel* it is. For example, if you feel that *my work* is extremely interesting, circle between interesting and boring like this:

Interesting (7) 6 5 4 3 2 1 Boring

On the other hand, if you feel that it is extremely boring, circle between interesting and boring like this:

Interesting 7 6 5 4 3 2 (1) Boring

However, if you feel neutral about *my work*, circle the number in the middle like this:

Interesting 7 6 5 (4) 3 2 1 Boring

The Questionnaire

Important:

1. Be sure to respond to every scale for every phrase.

2. Do not make more than one response to a given scale for a given phrase.

3. The best answers are your first impressions, so do not puzzle over items.

MYSELF AS A DISCUSSION LEADER
(e.g., in a laboratory or seminar)

1.	Organized	7	6	5	4	3	2	1	Disorganized
2.	Communicative	7	6	5	4	3	2	1	Uncommunicative
3.	Sketchy	1	2	3	4	5	6	7	Thorough
4.	Superior	7	6	5	4	3	2	1	Inferior

5.	Tense	1	2	3	4	5	6	7	Calm
6.	Articulate	7	6	5	4	3	2	1	Inarticulate
7.	Weak	1	2	3	4	5	6	7	Strong
8.	Insecure	1	2	3	4	5	6	7	Confident
9.	Prepared	7	6	5	4	3	2	1	Unprepared
10.	Coherent	7	6	5	4	3	2	1	Incoherent
11.	Unplanned	1	2	3	4	5	6	7	Planned
12.	Clear	7	6	5	4	3	2	1	Unclear

MYSELF AS A LECTURER

13.	Organized	7	6	5	4	3	2	1	Disorganized
14.	Communicative	7	6	5	4	3	2	1	Uncommunicative
15.	Sketchy	1	2	3	4	5	6	7	Thorough
16.	Superior	7	6	5	4	3	2	1	Inferior
17.	Tense	1	2	3	4	5	6	7	Calm
18.	Articulate	7	6	5	4	3	2	1	Inarticulate
19.	Weak	1	2	3	4	5	6	7	Strong
20.	Insecure	1	2	3	4	5	6	7	Confident
21.	Prepared	7	6	5	4	3	2	1	Unprepared
22.	Coherent	7	6	5	4	3	2	1	Incoherent
23.	Unplanned	1	2	3	4	5	6	7	Planned
24.	Clear	7	6	5	4	3	2	1	Unclear

MYSELF AS A TUTOR
(working with an individual student as advisor, supervisor, etc.)

25. Organized	7	6	5	4	3	2	1	Disorganized
26. Communicative	7	6	5	4	3	2	1	Uncommunicative
27. Sketchy	1	2	3	4	5	6	7	Thorough
28. Superior	7	6	5	4	3	2	1	Inferior
29. Tense	1	2	3	4	5	6	7	Calm
30. Articulate	7	6	5	4	3	2	1	Inarticulate
31. Weak	1	2	3	4	5	6	7	Strong
32. Insecure	1	2	3	4	5	6	7	Confident
33. Prepared	7	6	5	4	3	2	1	Unprepared
34. Coherent	7	6	5	4	3	2	1	Incoherent
35. Unplanned	1	2	3	4	5	6	7	Planned
36. Clear	7	6	5	4	3	2	1	Unclear

Scoring Key: Questionnaire (1)

1. Myself as a discussion leader
   a. For a total score in organization add your ratings in the rows specified:
   #1 _____
   #3 _____
   #9 _____
   #11 _____
   Total _____
   Mean score: Divide by 4 = _____
   b. For a total score in communication add your ratings in the rows specified:
   #2 _____
   #6 _____
   #10 _____
   #12 _____

Total _____
Mean score: Divide total by 4 = _____

c. For a total score in confidence add your ratings in the rows specified:
    #4 _____
    #5 _____
    #7 _____
    #8 _____
    Total _____
    Mean score: Divide total by 4 = _____

2. Myself as a lecturer
  a. For a total score in organization add your ratings in the rows specified:
    #13 _____
    #15 _____
    #21 _____
    #23 _____
    Total _____
    Mean score: Divide total by 4 = _____

  b. For a total score in communication add your ratings in the rows specified:
    #14 _____
    #18 _____
    #22 _____
    #24 _____
    Total _____
    Mean score: Divide total by 4= _____

  c. For a total score in confidence add your ratings in the rows specified:
    #16 _____
    #17 _____
    #19 _____
    #20 _____
    Total _____
    Mean score: Divide total by 4= _____

3. Myself as a tutor
  a. For a total score in organization add your ratings in the rows specified:
    #25 _____
    #27 _____
    #33 _____
    #35 _____

Total
Mean score: Divide total by 4= _____

b. For a total score in communication add your ratings in the rows specified:

#26   _____
#30   _____
#34   _____
#36   _____
Total   _____
Mean score: Divide total by 4= _____

c. For a total score in confidence add your ratings in the rows specified:

#28   _____
#29   _____
#31   _____
#32   _____
Total   _____
Mean score: Divide total by 4= _____

Summary Sheet: Questionnaire (1)

Complete this summary sheet by writing your mean scores in the appropriate spaces:

	DISCUSSION LEADER	LECTURER	TUTOR
Organization	_____	_____	_____
Ability to communicate	_____	_____	_____
Confidence	_____	_____	_____

Your scores are a reflection of how you perceive yourself. You will find it useful to compare your mean scores in each category to see if your confidence matches your perceived ability to communicate and degree of organization. You can also assess the teaching mode in which you are most organized, communicative, and confident.

The following key serves as a guide for interpretation:

MEAN SCORE	YOUR PERCEPTION OF YOURSELF
6.1-7.0	Extremely organized, communicative, confident
4.6-6.0	Fairly organized, communicative, confident
3.6-4.5	Average in organization, communication, confidence
2.1-3.5	Lacking in organization, communication, confidence
1.0-2.0	Very poor in organization, communication, confidence

Self-Assessment Questionnaire (2)

Below are 18 statements related to your feelings during the preparation and delivery and after the conclusion of a lecture. You are asked to rate yourself as to how often each statement applies to you by circling the appropriate word [for example, (5) Never].

1. Audiences seem bored when I speak.

    (5) Never   (4) Rarely   (3) Sometimes   (2) Usually   (1) Always

2. The prospect of facing an audience arouses in me feelings of apprehension.

    (5) Never   (4) Rarely   (3) Sometimes   (2) Usually   (1) Always

3. While preparing a speech I am in a constant state of anxiety.

    (5) Never   (4) Rarely   (3) Sometimes   (2) Usually   (1) Always

4. I dislike using my body and voice expressively.

    (5) Never   (4) Rarely   (3) Sometimes   (2) Usually   (1) Always

5. It is difficult for me to calmly search my mind for the right word to express   my thoughts while lecturing.

(5) Never   (4) Rarely   (3) Sometimes   (2) Usually   (1) Always

6. I am in a state of nervous tension after delivering a lecture.

(5) Never   (4) Rarely   (3) Sometimes   (2) Usually   (1) Always

7. I lose confidence if I find the audience is not interested in my speech.

(5) Never   (4) Rarely   (3) Sometimes   (2) Usually   (1) Always

8. At the conclusion of the lecture I feel that I have failed.

(5) Never   (4) Rarely   (3) Sometimes   (2) Usually   (1) Always

9. I feel elated after addressing a group.

(5) Always   (4) Usually   (3) Sometimes   (2) Rarely   (1) Never

10. I enjoy preparing my lectures.

(5) Always   (4) Usually   (3) Sometimes   (2) Rarely   (1) Never

11. I feel relaxed and comfortable while speaking.

(5) Always   (4) Usually   (3) Sometimes   (2) Rarely   (1) Never

12. Although I am nervous just before getting up, I soon forget my fears and enjoy   the experience.

(5) Always   (4) Usually   (3) Sometimes   (2) Rarely   (1) Never

13. I feel satisfied at the conclusion of the lecture.

(5) Always   (4) Usually   (3) Sometimes   (2) Rarely   (1) Never

14. At the conclusion of a lecture I feel that I have had a pleasant experience.

(5) Always   (4) Usually   (3) Sometimes   (2) Rarely   (1) Never

15. New and pertinent ideas come to me as I am planning a lecture.

(5) Always   (4) Usually   (3) Sometimes   (2) Rarely   (1) Never

16. I feel that I can't get things organized before I lecture.

(5) Never   (4) Rarely   (3) Sometimes   (2) Usually   (1) Always

17. I have a hard time arranging what I want to say into an organized lecture.

(5) Never   (4) Rarely   (3) Sometimes   (2) Usually   (1) Always

18. When I finish my lecture I feel that my ideas got across well.

(5) Always   (4) Usually   (3) Sometimes   (2) Rarely   (1) Never

Scoring Key: Questionnaire (2)

This self-assessment questionnaire provides data about how you feel while preparing and delivery and after completing your lecture. Mean scores should be calculated by adding your ratings from the questions which are indicates (write in the numbers which you circled).

1. Preparing a lecture
    #2   _____
    #3   _____
    #10   _____
    #15   _____

#16   _____
#17   _____
Total _____
Mean score: Divide total by 6= _____

2. Delivering a lecture
    #1   _____
    #4   _____
    #5   _____
    #7   _____
    #11   _____
    #12   _____
    Total _____
    Mean score: Divide total by 6= _____

3. After a lecture
    #6   _____
    #8   _____
    #9   _____
    #13   _____
    #14   _____
    #18   _____
    Total _____
    Mean score: Divide total by 6= _____

Your scores are only a reflection of how you perceive yourself. You will find it useful to compare your mean scores in each category.

The following key can serve as a general guide for interpretation:

MEAN SCORE	YOUR PERCEPTION OF YOURSELF
4.1-5.0	Very confident
3.1-4.0	Somewhat confident
2.1-3.0	Somewhat tense or unsure
1.0-2.0	Very tense or unsure

LESSON PLAN

Goal- To examine characteristics and skills that exemplify good teaching and determine strategies to acquire them.

Objectives:
To name 10 characteristics of good teaching.
To develop awareness of skills of a good teacher.
To determine own teaching strengths.
To practice ways of improving.

Pre-Opening
Make this provocative statement and discuss group's reaction:
"Good teachers are born, not made."

I. Introduction
Today we will discuss characteristics of good teaching, identify your personal assets as a teacher, and provide suggestions for how teachers can develop excellence in the classroom. This is important because good teaching influences students' learning.

At the conclusion of this session, you will have an understanding of which characteristics are essential in each of three areas: Personal, Intellectual, and Instructional. You will also gain ideas on how you can personally take action to improve your teaching skills.

"How can we quantify good teaching?"

Think of one teacher who has had a positive impact on you. Memories of this relationship can provide valuable insight into effective teaching. Use these memories as personal guides and emulate that teacher.

"What characteristics did the teacher have that made an impression on you?"

"Why develop characteristics of good teaching?" What difference does it make?"

II. Body
Identify five things you excel at in the classroom.

After completing the self-assessment instruments included, what areas did you identify for improvement?

Group discussion:

How can teachers develop excellence?

How can teachers overcome the pet peeves identified by students?

What makes a good teacher?

Divide participants into three groups. Assign group #1 to identify characteristics in the Personal area that are essential to good teaching; group #2, identify characteristics in the Intellectual area, and group #3, identify characteristics in the Instructional area. Indicate each group will name a recorder who will report results to the group at large after discussion (15-25 minutes).

III. Conclusion

Have participants demonstrate characteristics of good teaching.

Review objectives of session and key points covered during session.

Have participants summarize why good teaching is essential, what constitutes good teaching (what are the characteristics teachers possess?), and how teachers can develop excellence.

"There is no substitute for a good teacher."

Resources:

Self-Assessment Instruments from chapter.

WORKSHEET

"I am most effective as a teacher when ..."

Do you think teaching requires both art and science? Explain.

Think back to the last time you were a student. What characteristics did the teacher have that appealed to you?

What things did the teacher do that did NOT appeal to you?

Were they personality issues or did they interfere with your learning?

What is your greatest teaching asset?

What are characteristics of good teaching?

What characteristic can you develop in the personal area, the intellectual area, and the instructional area?

Chapter 7

SKILL DEVELOPMENT

"There are no secrets to success. It is the result of preparation, hard work, learning from failure."

- Gen. Colin L. Powell
The Black Collegian

Now that you have an understanding of the foundations on which teaching and learning is built, you can turn your attention to the more tangible work of teaching. This begins with a planning phase where decisions are made on what content to teach, how to organize it, write objectives, and determine forms of evaluation. How to deliver the information using a variety of methods and resources and prepare a syllabus complete this planning phase by committing details to paper, thereby making it tangible and real.

PLANNING

A large percentage of your time in the planning phase is used to develop the curriculum. In addition to identifying content, you will also need to develop objectives, decide which teaching methods to use, determine what other resources and materials you need, and consider the evaluation you will use. This all occurs before you step into a presentation or class session.

Zero in on the purpose of your session. Identify the major topic which will be the focus of the session, and the general objectives. Next determine all the subtopics that relate to the major topic. For example if the topic is FRUIT, subtopics include apples, oranges, bananas. Depending on the time available, you may decide that discussing those three fruits is all that time permits. You need to determine what information to include about each of the three fruits. For example, how and where they are grown, common ways of eating them, ways of cooking them, or what vitamins they each provide and for what purpose in our bodies. What to include must fit with the purpose you have determined. At this point, appropriate content is identified, and some content is eliminated.

Grappling with these questions will propel you into the next phase. That is, you cannot answer these questions without first determining what the specific objectives are for this session on fruit. More information on writing objectives follows.

Now you can decide which teaching methods are best suited to convey the information and allow students to achieve the objectives. There are several choices and an indepth description of teaching methods follows. After determining methods, decide what materials or resources you need to carry out each method.

Evaluation methods also are determined. This is an important planning step because the learning objectives, the teaching methods and the evaluation method must all be in harmony. If competencies are identified, delineate which skills you want students to demonstrate. Consider if the outcome you want students to achieve is in the area of skills, knowledge, or attitudes. How you measure the outcomes is impacted by those three areas of learning.

CURRICULUM DESIGN

Writing the content for the curriculum can be illustrated using a funnel. Use the curriculum diagram at the end of this chapter as a planning chart.

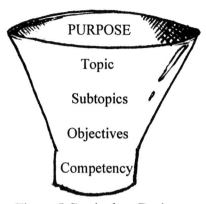

Figure 5 Curriculum Design

Fisch (1988) suggested that when faculty are designing instruction, instead of asking, "What should I include?", faculty should ask, "How much can I, or should I leave out?"

He uses the example of trying to direct a driver from Lexington to Indianapolis. "Would you provide a series of aerial photographs, carefully taped together and marked with the route? Of course not; that much detail severely detracts from your purpose. Instead, you provide a map that represents the route in a schematic way. Better still, you take a sheet of paper, sketch on it two lines at right angles to each other, label them I-64 and I-65, and add a couple of arrows, along with circles identified as Shelbyville, Louisville and Columbus to help orient the driver.

Students are not likely to become independent learners if you give them all the information on a topic and then interpret and analyze it for them; you have done their thinking for them. Carefully determine how much you can leave out. Students have to learn to identify what additional information they need to problem solve and make decisions."

WRITING OBJECTIVES

Instructional objectives are designed to identify the intended outcomes of the learning experience. The objectives answer the question of what it is you want the students to be able to know, think, or do at the end of the session, or the course. These three areas are also known as the cognitive, affective, and psychomotor domains. Objectives can be written in each of these three domains using a taxonomy or classification system. Refer to page 140 at the end of this chapter.

Cognitive objectives are written in a hierarchy of intellectual outcomes. They are the easiest to write and therefore, the most commonly used. Outcomes involve either recall or recognition of the learned material. Affective objectives are hierarchial in an order from receiving stimuli to forming values. These are the most difficult because of the vagueness, and often the outcome is hard to observe. The outcome behavior often needs to be inferred. Psychomotor objectives are written using a hierarchy of responses leading to movement. These objectives are easily observed by noting action, and demonstration of the skill is frequently the method of evaluation used. The box on page 135 depicts a summary of outcomes in the areas of cognitive (knowledge), affective, and psychomotor (performance).

There are several purposes of objectives. They:
are useful tools in the design, implementation and evaluation of the instruction
convey instructional intent and expectations to the students
provide a guide for the student
provide direction to the instructor
assist in the selection of teaching methods
help in determining subject matter or course content
are useful in deciding what resources will augment the instruction i.e. audio visuals, handouts
assist in test construction or outcome assessment

Three areas that affect objective writing are: subject matter, teaching material (equipment) and methods.

A key point to keep in mind when writing objectives is that they are written in terms of what the *student* will know, think, or do. They are NOT written based on what the teacher does.

Objectives begin with an action verb. Good examples are provided at the end of this chapter, page 128.

To determine the appropriateness of the objectives written, use sample test items to see how closely the objectives align with the proposed assessment.

Ask yourself these questions about the objectives you have written.

Are they realistic, relevant and attainable?
Does each objective began with a verb that indicates activity on the part of the student?
Is each objective stated in terms of student performance?
Is each objective written as a learning product?
What student behavior is expected as a result of the learning experience?
Are the objectives reflective of and representative of course topics?

When you write objectives, remember the SMART principle:

S - are objectives specific?
M - are objectives measurable?
A - are objectives achievable?
R - are objectives relevant?
T - are objectives time-framed?

In summary, good objectives answer three questions:

What is the learner able to do? (performance)
Under what conditions will the learner perform? (condition)
How well must it be done? (criterion)

TEACHING METHODS

HOW DO YOU DECIDE?

Now you can identify which teaching methods to use that best support the content, the objectives, the learners, and the outcome assessment. This is an important step in curriculum planning, yet it is often overlooked. I recommend using a minimum of two different methods for each hour session. No one teaching method has been determine to be the best. Students learn in different ways, therefore no one method will reach all of them. Using at least two different methods will reach a broader segment of students. Additionally, students' attention spans are limited, usually 15-20 minutes. One way to hold their attention is to shift to a different teaching method every 15-20 minutes.

Here are some of the considerations in choosing teaching methods that will convey the intention best.

1. *Interaction with audience* What level of interplay is possible? The size of the group is one consideration. Class size over 30 requires careful management and special considerations for most methods beyond the lecture. Ways to increase the amount of interaction can be accomplished in the following ways:

Use a flip chart, a video, or other form of audio visual to provide interaction between it and the teacher.
Two teachers or speakers in a debate or interview increases the interaction, but only in the front of the room. Conduct a panel discussion, or a demonstration to add even more.
To increase interaction between the teacher and the students, or the group in the case of a presentation, an easy technique is to allow questions to be asked.
Groups can be divided into listening teams or responsive groups. The presenter gives each group an assignment (something to listen for during the session) and the group provides a reaction.
Maximum interaction between students is achieved by using buzz groups, learning cells, dyads, triads, or small groups of four or more people. These smaller divisions huddle and offer a verbal response after the interaction.

2. *Time* How much time do you have to convey the information and what pace is necessary? Is it a one time block or is it a serial format where you have additional sessions with the group? You will also consider how much preparation time is needed by you for the various teaching methods.

Here are some examples:
1. Presentation - purpose to give information

Method	Time to Develop	Cost	Passive/Active
Lecture	High	Low	P
Lecturette	High	Low	P
Microteaching	High	Low	P/A
Debate	Med	Low	P/A

2. Demonstration - purpose to acquire skill

Showing	High	Low	P
Coaching	Low	Low	A/P
Rehearsing	Low	Low	A/P

3. Group Learning - purpose to gain knowledge

Skills practice	High	Low	A
Discussion	Low	Low	A
Structured Discussion	Med	Low	A
Panel	Med	Low	A/P
Seminar	Med	Low	A
Brainstorming	Low	Low	A
Buzz groups	Low	Low	A
Problem-solving group	Med	Low	A
Learning/teaching team	Med	Low	A

4. Individual learning

Reading	High	Low	P

Method	Time to Develop	Cost	Passive/Active

5. Structured Experiences

Role Play	High	High/Med	A
Drama	High	Low	A
Case Study	High	Med	A
In-basket	High	Med	A/P
Exercises	High	Low/Med	A

Taken from: Loughary & Hopson (1979).

3. *Resources* What will supplement your presentation? What budget is available for materials? Consider what kind of audio visuals will support the content, is a field trip possible, what equipment or props can be used to enhance the learning experience?

4. Your *ability and style* are factors in deciding which teaching methods to use. This is an important component of curriculum planning, yet it is often overlooked. Determine how skillful and comfortable you are with various methods. Decide if your role is to convey information, to guide the student, or to demonstrate a skill.

5. What are the *objectives*? Refer to later section on objectives and the nature of the learning task.

6. What method of *evaluation* will you use? If your teaching method encourages group participation, group projects and group activities, all or some of your evaluation needs to be based on the student's contribution to the group. If your purpose is to convey facts and information, a true and false examination is suitable.

If the goal is for students to gain a skill, can students demonstrate their ability?

Based on the desired outcome, here is a guide for selecting an appropriate teaching method.

Outcome   *Method*

Knowledge -   Lecture, television, debate, dialogue, panel, speech, reading, or symposium.

Application -   Demonstration, Socratic dialogue, problem-solving
                discussion, case discussion, audience participation.
Skills -   Role playing, case discussion, demonstration,
                simulations, coaching.
Attitudes -   Role playing, buzz groups, experience-sharing
                discussion.
Values -   Debate, drama, guided discussion, role playing, lecture.

7. What *environment* will you be in? How can you make the
    experience physically and psychologically comfortable? What is
    the room arrangement? Refer to seating arrangement at the end of
    this chapter for possible room arrangements.

In summary, the major categories of teaching methods are:

a) Instructor-centered (teacher is primarily responsible for conveying
    information) - lecture, demonstration, questioning
b) Interactive (promotes communication and participation between
    students and teacher) - group discussion, group projects, peer
    teaching
c) Individual (allows students to pursue learning at different paces and
    levels of ability) - computer-aided instruction, self-pace modules,
    reading
d) Experiential (affords students opportunities to experience real or
    simulated learning situations with supervision and feedback) - field
    trips, laboratories, role play, simulations, drill (practice)

WHAT ARE THE CHOICES?

Understanding the advantages and disadvantages of teaching methods is
helpful to assist you with the decision of which methods to use. Methods
reviewed here are lectures, brainstorming, role play, case discussion,
simulations, and demonstrations. Additional information on groups is in
Chapter 8.

Lecture is the most common teaching method. It typically involves a
one-way communication with information from the teacher to the
students. It is a passive form of learning for the students. It is time

efficient when conveying large volumes of factual information. For large groups, the lecture method lowers the teacher/student ratio. Additional information on lectures is in Chapter 9.

Brainstorming is a method introduced in 1920 by Walt Disney, known as one of the most creative people to exist. It is a method based on the premise that more ideas are generated if participants are allowed to do creative thinking before judgmental thinking occurs. This process supports Disney's concept that everyone has a natural ability to be creative, but often we block ourselves and creativity is stifled.

This method involves identifying a topic or a problem to solve for a group of people. Everyone is asked to reflect for a short time, and then to verbally "call out" any thoughts. Someone volunteers to write all ideas on the board. Ideas are not screened and no one is allowed to offer any judgment. Everything is fair game. Practical considerations are not important during the exercise. The more ideas discovered, the greater likelihood that a solution or an answer will be uncovered. Often one person's remark will trigger another idea from someone else. This concept is called "piggy backing" or "hitch hiking" and is encouraged. Interesting combinations can emerge. There is a theory that at least 17 responses need to be recorded in order to increase the probability that a workable, useful idea will emerge. After all ideas are exhausted, discussion and evaluation occur.

Advantages of using this method are that it is very low risk because no value or judgment on the ideas is made as they are generated. This free wheeling allows for the creative process to occur. Everyone is encouraged to participate because everyone has ideas. This spontaneous expression produces a quantity of ideas. It is an opportunity for the teacher to discover what people already know. This method takes virtually no preparation time and there is no cost associated with it. Additionally, this method produces a lot of ideas in a short period of time in a way that is stimulating and interesting for students.

Role play was a method demonstrated by J.L. Moreno in 1933 in the setting of psychodrama. This method sparks emotion, connecting the intellectual experience with the emotional. Students act out a situation or problem. It helps them explore feelings and allows them to practice skills. For example, in medical education, various doctor/patient scenarios are used to determine how the doctor can handle certain situations. After the role play is completed, discussion ensues whereby other student observers suggest how they would handle the situation and explain why they would do it the same or differently. Role play makes a strong visual impact. It is highly engaging, not just for the "play actors" but also for the students observing the action. It is hard to ignore because of the action component. Value is added from this dramatic impact. Players are encouraged to encounter role reversal situation as in the doctor playing the patient to develop empathy. The players can also use the techniques of mirroring where a character moves in and translates what the player said into what was really meant, or alter ego where an inner voice speaks.

Group Discussion is the method that typically uses a "case" for students to dissect. Case studies were used as a teaching method by Harvard University in the 1950s. Group discussion is the format where students work through real situations where they pull apart data, study it, make a decision on what to do after the group's discussion, and various options are revealed. It is a vehicle that brings real world reality into the classroom. This method is very effective in situations where there is no one right answer and in situations where there is no black and white. It is often used in medicine, law, and is finally catching on in teaching.

Students take diverse, fragmented material and put it together in a way that makes sense. They take data, analyze and evaluate it, add judgment, make a decision, and then communicate it.

Advantages of using a case that is well-written and exciting, are that it holds the interest of students and encourages participation by each member. Students are able to develop interpersonal skills and often a change in attitudes via peer pressure. Students learn to accept feedback from peers. This method of case discussion also fosters critical thinking because each person must justify his/her position on an issue. Through the process, students are aided in decision making.

Successful use of case studies involves the coordination of the case material and objectives, preparation and participation by the students, and the facilitation skills of the leader. Cases need to be self contained and describe situations students can relate to. The use of cases and the group discussion method involves risk taking initially by teachers and learners. The case method requires a substantial investment in resources and in some instances, it may be more difficult to evaluate and assess outcomes compared to other methods. Chapter 8 presents an indepth coverage of group discussion and facilitating learning.

Simulations are another teaching method. Students engage in activities, or "games". They experience a situation similar to what they will be faced with in real life or in future careers, using carefully constructed, yet controlled situations. Preparation by the leader is required. This method has the advantage of creating a safe environment for people to experience situations that involve some risk without experiencing harsh consequences.

Demonstration is the final major teaching method described. Demonstrations are frequently used in laboratory settings. In this method, the teacher shows a group of students how to do something. For example, using a stethoscope may initially be demonstrated by a competent doctor in a step by step manner. Students observe the steps, and notice proper procedures and/or correct techniques. The instructor may demonstrate the procedure more than once to insure students grasp the principles and important points. Students then have an opportunity to use, in this case, the stethoscope. They practice using it, as often as needed until an assessment by the instructor determines they have acquired the desired skills and are competent to use the equipment. Demonstrations are also used as a teaching method when enough equipment is not available for all students to engage in the actual "doing." They do, however, benefit from the experience of observation, and/or some limited practice time.

SYLLABUS CONSTRUCTION

A well constructed syllabus is organized and conveys a great deal of information to the students. A high quality syllabus is essential to clarify students' expectations about active learning and reduce students' anxiety.

Absolute basics for a syllabus include an outline of class dates, topics, and reading assignments. The official course title and number, any prerequisites, the instructor's name, office hours, and phone number, where and when the course meets are included. Any required texts and supplies are indicated on the syllabus.

A quality syllabus will offer a cover sheet that clearly spells out your expectations for students and indicates their responsibilities for the class. The cover sheet carries a statement of your philosophy on the teaching/learning experience. It also includes an overview of the course and identifies explicitly the course objectives and outcomes. The assessment and/or grading is also revealed. The class format is described, and certain key dates are noted so students are alert to when assignments are due. You may need to state pertinent information about academic policies and procedures at your school such as attendance and make-up assignments.

Hopefully your experience with students is different, but often when students receive the syllabus the first day of class, they file it away and only look at it as a desperate last maneuver before exams or assignments are rumored to be due. Consider using the following activity to make the syllabus come alive.

Have students form groups of five to seven students, randomly assigned. Give the groups the following information (write it on the board or an overhead for clarity):

1. Select a spokesperson (the student whose last name is nearest the end of the alphabet).
2. Each group critiques the syllabus using one or two items, depending on how many groups you have.

> evaluate the grading system
> evaluate the assignments
> clarify the expectations the teacher has of the students
> state the responsibilities of the students
> critique the relevancy of the topics
> highlight important dates when tests, papers, projects are due

At the end of a designated time period, students come back together. Each group spokesperson introduces the group members and then relays the information generated from their assigned topic. Students can get to know each other right from the start, and there should be no misunderstanding about what will happen in the course.

The planning phase commits information to paper. Developing curriculum is a process of deciding what content will be included, planning the topics and subtopics based on the objectives to be fulfilled, and determining how the content will be evaluated. Selecting which teaching methods can be a complex process because of the variety available, and because of the variables of audience, time available, environment designated for the session, the objectives and the nature of the content, and the teacher's skill and comfort level with the various methods. Improving the teacher's skill is an area where change can occur.

After reviewing what needs to be done, decisions are made on how the educational process will be managed, and this information is organized into a written syllabus. This document becomes the skeleton of the entire educational experience. A good syllabus contains information to guide students and reduces the amount of time the teacher spends repeating standard information such as phone and office of the teacher, reading and other assignments, and important due dates for tests or assignments. However, pertinent information about objectives, evaluation, and philosophy can be verbally reinforced for the students to clarify expectations and reduce misunderstandings.

You are now prepared to conduct an in-depth investigation of several teaching methods. You can make intelligent decisions related to which methods to use for various purposes, and you will confidently acquire the skills and techniques to use them effectively.

"Every good teacher learns as he/she teaches. This indeed is one of the miracles of teaching; it is not a form of exchange in which the teacher loses what the student gains, but an extraordinary active development in which, after the class, not only the student knows more, but the teacher knows more."

- Kenneth Boulding

CURRICULUM DESIGN

Title of Course/Presentation _____ Hours _____

Content Topics	Objectives	Teaching Methods	Faculty/Resource	Time Frame	Assessment	Competency
List each topic area to be covered	List objectives	Describe the teaching method(s) used for each.	List the faculty person or presenter for each topic.	State the time needed for the topic area.	Identify how student knowledge or skill level relative to topic will be measured.	State the competency topic addresses.

VERBS FOR OBJECTIVES

The verbs listed below, although not inclusive, will assist you in writing objectives.

KNOWLEDGE   COMPREHENSION APPLICATION

KNOWLEDGE	COMPREHENSION	APPLICATION
Annotate	Cite	Apply
Answer	Describe	Assemble
Compile	Discuss	Build
Define	Explain	Demonstrate
List	Express	Employ
Match	Identify	Illustrate
Name	Locate	Interpret
Recall	Outline	Make
Recite	Paraphrase	Operate
Record	Report	Practice
Repeat	Restate	Schedule
	Review	Sketch
	Tell	Translate
	Write	Use

ANALYSIS   SYNTHESIS   EVALUATION

ANALYSIS	SYNTHESIS	EVALUATION
Analyze	Arrange	Appraise
Calculate	Assemble	Assess
Categorize	Collect	Choose
Compare	Compose	Evaluate
Criticize	Create	Judge
Debate	Design/Graph/Plot	Measure
Diagram	Enumerate	Rank
Differentiate	Extrapolate	Rate
Distinguish	Formulate	Revise
Estimate	Generate	Score

Experiment	Manage	Select
Inspect	Organize	
Inventory	Plan	
Question	Prepare	
Relate	Propose	
Solve	Setup	
	Summarize	

Preparing and Using Instructional Objectives

TYPES OF LEARNING OUTCOMES COMMON TO MANY AREAS AND LEVELS OF INSTRUCTION

Lower Level Cognitive

Outcomes

   Knowledge of

   Comprehension of

   Application of

Terms

Facts

Symbols

Rules

Concepts

Principles

Procedures

Higher Level Thinking

Skills

   Analysis

   Synthesis

   Evaluation

Identifying

Distinguishing between

Inferring

Relating

Formulating

Generating

Judging

Affective Outcomes		Social
Attitudes		Personal
Interests	{	Scientific
Appreciations		Educational
Adjustments		Vocational
		Art, Music, Literature

Performance Outcomes		Speaking
Procedure		Singing
Product	{	Drawing
Procedure and product		Computing
		Writing
		Laboratory skills
		Research skills
		Vocational skills
		Musical skills
		Physical skills

Gronlund, Norman E., *How to Write and Use Instructional Objectives*, 1991 4/e   Used with permission of Prentice Hall, Upper Saddle River, NJ.

TABLE I. Major Categories in the Cognitive Domain of the Taxonomy of Educational Objectives (Bloom, 1956)

Descriptions of the Major Categories in the Cognitive Domain

1. **Knowledge.** Knowledge is defined as the remembering of previously learned material. This may involve the recall of a wide range of material, from specific facts to complete theories, but all that is required is the bringing to mind of the appropriate information. Knowledge represents the lowest level of learning outcomes in the cognitive domain.

2. **Comprehension.** Comprehension is defined as the ability to grasp the meaning of material. This may be shown by translating material from one form to another (words by numbers), by interpreting material (explaining or summarizing), and by estimating future trends (predicting consequences or effects). These learning outcomes go one step beyond the simple remembering of material, and represent the lowest level of understanding.

3. **Application.** Application refers to the ability to use learned material in new and concrete situations. This may include the application of such things as rules, methods, concepts, principles, laws, and theories. Learning outcomes in this area require a higher level of understanding than those under comprehension.

4. **Analysis.** Analysis refers to the ability to break down material into its component parts so that its organizational structure may be understood. This may include the identification of the parts, analysis of the relationships between parts, and recognition of the organizational principles involved. Learning outcomes here represent a higher intellectual level than comprehension and application cause they require an understanding of both the content and the structural form of the material.

5. **Synthesis.** Synthesis refers to the ability to put parts together to form a new whole. This may involve the production of a unique communication (theme or speech), or plan of operations (research proposal), or a set of abstract relations (scheme for classifying information). Learning outcomes in this area stress creative behaviors, with major emphasis on the formulation of new patterns of structures.

6. **Evaluation.** Evaluation is concerned with the ability to judge the value of material (statement, novel, poem, research report) for a given purpose. The judgments are to be based on definite criteria. These may be internal criteria

(organization) or external criteria (relevance to the purpose), and the student may determine the criteria or be given them. Learning outcomes in this area are highest in the cognitive hierarchy because they contain elements of all of the other categories, plus conscious value judgments based on clearly defined criteria.

TABLE II. Examples of General Instructional Objectives and Clarifying Verbs for the Cognitive Domain of the Taxonomy

Illustrative General Instructional Objectives	Illustrative Verbs for Stating Specific Learning Outcomes
Knows common terms Knows specific facts Knows methods and procedures Knows basic concepts Knows principles	Defines, describes, identifies, labels, lists, matches, names, outlines, reproduces, selects, states
Understands facts and principles Interprets verbal material Interprets charts and graphs Translates verbal material to mathematical formulas Estimates future consequences implied in data Justifies methods and procedures	Converts, defends, distinguishes, estimates, explains, extends, generalizes, gives examples, infers, paraphrases, predicts, rewrites, summarizes
Applies concepts and principles to new situations Applies laws and theories to practical situations Solves mathematical problems Constructs charts and graphs Demonstrates correct usage of a method or procedure	Changes, computes, demonstrates, discovers, manipulates, modifies, operates, predicts, prepares, produces, relates, shows, solves, uses

Recognizes unstated assumptions Recognizes logical fallacies in reasoning Distinguishes between facts and inferences Evaluates the relevancy of data Analyzes the organizational structure of a work (art, music, writing)	Breaks down, diagrams, differentiates, discriminates, distinguishes, identifies, illustrates, infers, outlines, points out, relates, selects, separates, subdivides
Writes a well-organized theme Gives a well-organized speech Writes a creative short story (or poem, or music) Proposes a plan for an experiment Integrates learning from different areas into a plan for solving a problem Formulates a new scheme for classifying objects (or events, or ideas)	Categorizes, combines, compiles, composes, creates, devises, designs, explains, generates, modifies, organizes, plans, rearranges, reconstructs, relates, reorganizes, revises, rewrites, summarizes, tells, writes
Judges the logical consistency of written material Judges the adequacy with which conclusions are supported by data Judges the value of a work (art, music, writing) by use of internal criteria Judges the value of a work (art, music, writing) by use of external standards of excellence	Appraisers, compares, concludes contrasts, criticizes, describes, discriminates, explains, justifies, interprets, relates, summarizes, supports

TABLE III. Major Categories in the Affective Domain of the Taxonomy of Educational Objectives (Krathwohl, 1964)

Descriptions of the Major Categories in the Affective Domain

1. Receiving. Receiving refers to the student's willingness to attend to particular phenomena or stimuli (classroom activities, textbook, music, etc.). From a teaching standpoint, it is concerned with getting, holding, and directing the student's attention. Learning outcomes in this area range from the simple awareness that a thing exists to selective attention on the part of the learner. Receiving represents the lowest level of learning outcomes in the affective domain.

2. Responding. Responding refers to active participation on the part of the student. At this level he or she not only attends to a particular phenomenon but also reacts to it in some way. Learning outcomes in this area may emphasize acquiescence in responding (reads assigned material), willingness to respond (voluntarily reads beyond assignment), or satisfaction in responding (reads for pleasure or enjoyment). The higher levels of this category include those instructional objectives that are commonly classified under "interest"; that is, those that stress the seeking out and enjoyment of particular activities.

3. Valuing. Valuing is concerned with the worth or value a student attaches to a particular object, phenomenon, or behavior. This ranges in degree from the more simple acceptance of a value (desires to improve group skills) to the more complex level of commitment (assumes responsibility for the effective functioning of the group). Valuing is based on the internalization of a set of specified values, but clues to these values are expressed in the student's overt behavior. Learning outcomes in this area are concerned with behavior that is consistent and stable enough to make the value clearly identifiable. Instructional objectives that are commonly classified under "attitudes" and "appreciation" would fall into this category.

4. Organization. Organization is concerned with bringing together different values, resolving conflicts between them, and beginning the building of an internally consistent value system. Thus the emphasis is on comparing, relating, and synthesizing values. Learning outcomes may be concerned with the conceptualization of a value (recognizes the responsibility of each individual for improving human relations) or with the organization of a value system (develops a vocational plan that satisfies his or her need for both economic security and social service). Instructional objectives relating to the development of a philosophy of life would fall into this category.

5. Characterization by a Value or Value Complex. At this level of the affective domain the individual has a value system that has controlled his or her behavior for a sufficiently long time for him or her to have developed a characteristic "life-style." Thus the behavior is pervasive, consistent, and predictable. Learning outcomes at this level cover a broad range of activities, but the major emphasis is on the fact that the behavior is typical or characteristic of the student. Instructional objectives that are concerned with the student's general patterns of adjustment (personal, social, emotional) would be appropriate here.

TABLE IV. Examples of General Instructional Objectives and Clarifying Verbs for the Affective Domain of the Taxonomy

Illustrative General Instructional Objectives	Illustrative Verbs for Stating Specific Learning Outcomes
Listens attentively	Asks, chooses, describes, follows, gives, holds, identifies, locates, names, points to, replies, selects, sits erect, uses
Shows awareness of the importance of learning	
Shows sensitivity to human needs and social problems	
Accepts differences of race and culture	
Attends closely to the classroom activities	
Completes assigned homework	Answers, assists, complies, conforms, discusses, greets, helps, labels, performs, practices, presents, reads, recites, reports, selects, tells, writes
Obeys school rules	
Participates in class discussion	
Completes laboratory work	
Volunteers for special tasks	
Shows interest in subject	
Enjoys helping others	

Demonstrates belief in the democratic process	Completes, describes, differentiates, explains, follows, forms, initiates, invites, joins, justifies, proposes, reads, reports, selects, shares, studies, works
Appreciates good literature (art or music)	
Appreciates the role of science (or other subjects) in everyday life	
Shows concern for the welfare of others	
Demonstrates problem-solving attitude	
Demonstrates commitment to social improvement	
Recognizes the need for balance between freedom and responsibility in a democracy	Adheres, alters, arranges, combines, compares, completes, defends, explains, generalizes, identifies, integrates, modifies, orders, organize, prepares, relates, synthesizes
Recognizes the role of systematic planning in solving problems	
Accepts responsibility for his or her own behavior	
Understands and accepts his or her own strengths and limitations	
Formulates life plan in harmony with his or her abilities, interests, and beliefs	
Displays safety consciousness	Acts, discriminates, displays, influences, listens, modifies, performs, practices, proposes, qualifies, questions, revises, serves, solves, uses, verifies
Demonstrates self-reliance working independently	
Practices cooperation in group activities	
Uses objective approach in problem solving	
Demonstrates industry, punctuality, and self-discipline	
Maintains good health habits	

TABLE V. A Classification of Educational Objectives in the Psychomotor Domain (Simpson, 1972)

Description of the Major Categories in the Psychomotor Domain

1. Perception. The first level is concerned with the use of the sense organs to obtain cues that guide motor activity. This category ranges from sensory stimulation (awareness of a stimulus), through cue selection (selecting task-relevant cues), to translation (relating cue perception to action in a performance).

2. Set. Set refers to readiness to take a particular type of action. This category includes mental set (mental readiness to act), physical set (physical readiness to act), and emotional set (willingness to act). Perception of cues serves as an important prerequisite for this level.

3. Guided Response. Guided response is concerned with the early stages in learning a complex skill. It includes imitation (repeating an act demonstrated by the instructor) and trial and error (using a multiple-response approach to identify an appropriate response). Adequacy of performance is judged by an instructor or by a suitable set of criteria.

4. Mechanism. Mechanism is concerned with performance acts where the learned responses have become habitual and the movements can be performed with some confidence and proficiency. Learning outcomes at this level are concerned with performance skills of various types, but the movement patterns are less complex than at the next higher level.

5. Complex Overt Response. Complex overt response is concerned with the skillful performance of motor acts that involve complex movement patterns. Proficiency is indicated by a quick, smooth, accurate performance, requiring a minimum of energy. This category includes resolution of uncertainty (performs without hesitation) and automatic performance (movements are made with ease and good muscle control). Learning outcomes at this level include highly coordinated motor activities.

6. Adaptation. Adaptation is concerned with skills that are so well developed that the individual can modify movement patterns to fit special requirements or to meet a problem situation.

7. Origination. Origination refers to the creating of new movement patterns to fit a particular situation or specific problem. Learning outcomes at this level emphasize creativity based upon highly developed skills.

TABLE VI. Examples of General Instructional Objectives and Clarifying Verbs for the Psychomotor Domain

Illustrative General Instructional Objectives	Illustrative Verbs for Stating Specific Learning Outcomes
Recognizes malfunction by sound of machine Relates taste of food to need for reasoning Relates music to a particular dance step	Chooses, describes, detects, differentiates, distinguishes, identifies, isolates, relates, selects, separates
Knows sequence of steps in varnishing wood Demonstrates proper bodily stance for batting a ball Shows desire to type efficiently	Begins, displays, explains, moves, proceeds, reacts, responds, shows, starts, volunteers
Performs a golf swing as demonstrated Determines best sequence for preparing a meal	Assembles, builds, calibrates, constructs, dismantles, displays, dissects, fastens, fixes, grinds, heats, manipulates, measures, mends, mixes, organizes, sketches, works
Writes smoothly and legibly Sets up laboratory equipment Operates a slide projector Demonstrates a simple dance step	(Same list as for Guided Response)

Operates a power saw skillfully	(Same list as for Guided Response)
Demonstrates correct form in swimming	
Demonstrates skill in driving an automobile	
Performs skillfully on the violin	
Repairs electronic equipment quickly and accurately	
Adjusts tennis play to counteract opponent's style	Adapts, alters, changes, rearranges, reorganizes, revises, varies
Modifies swimming strokes to fit the roughness of the water	
Creates a dance step	Arranges, combines, composes, constructs, designs, originates
Creates a musical composition	
Designs a new dress style	

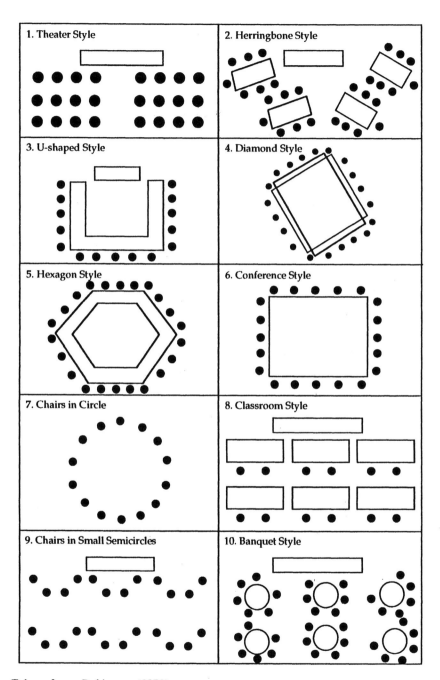

1. Theater Style

2. Herringbone Style

3. U-shaped Style

4. Diamond Style

5. Hexagon Style

6. Conference Style

7. Chairs in Circle

8. Classroom Style

9. Chairs in Small Semicircles

10. Banquet Style

Taken from Robinson (1979)

LESSON PLAN

Goal - To gain skill in planning what content to teach and in selecting delivery methods.

Objectives:
To design curriculum around content and organize it.
To write objectives.
To consider forms of evaluation to assess student learning.
To select delivery methods.

Pre-Opening:
Curriculum design is like taking a lot of tinkertoys and building them into one product. If time permits, divide into small groups, give them a few materials (duct tape, lifesavers, nails, tinker toys, etc.) and have group build a product.

I. Introduction

II. Body

Review process of curriculum design:
  Topic and Subtopic identification
  Develop an outline
  Enumerate objectives and method for evaluation
  Choose teaching methods
  Identify resources and materials needed
  Write syllabus

How do you decide on teaching methods?

What are the choices?

What are the advantages and disadvantages of each method?

Practice writing objectives. Use two verbs from each of the categories listed on page 138.

Complete the curriculum design guide on page for a class or session.

III. Conclusion

Review

Summarize

Resources:

WORKSHEET

How do you decide what to include in your teaching, a presentation, or a training session?

Develop an outline of this chapter.

What area of curriculum design do you need help with?

What do you include in a lesson plan?

Practice writing objectives using two verbs from each of the six categories listed on page 138.

Revamp or develop a new syllabus.

How will you introduce it to the students?

What teaching methods are available?

List three advantages and three disadvantages of each method.

What methods do you use most of the time, and why?

GROUP DISCUSSION

"You cannot teach anybody directly, only facilitate their learning."

- Carl Rogers

This chapter provides extensive information about group discussion, which is a method that facilitates student learning. It is the most common teaching method used to increase student participation, foster active learning, and encourage collaborative learning. However, it is often the most abused because the skills needed to be an effective facilitator require both a change in attitude and a change in technique. A facilitator guides the learning process, which requires taking on a role different than a traditional teacher who has knowledge and passes it along in a more direct way.

The necessary skills in both areas can be learned and it is important that teachers undertake the time and effort needed to broaden their teaching repertoire to successfully use group discussion. Students indicate a desire for vigorous class discussions as part of their learning. Group discussion is an effective way to stimulate student interest in the course, subject, or training.

Additionally, discussion is effective for retention if students can apply the information discussed to case studies, simulated or real work situations for purposes of decision-making and problem-solving. Students are able to develop skills, not just in discussing, debating, and justifying positions, but also in the broader communication skill areas of listening and observing.

One of the goals of active learning is to increase the student's participation in the learning process, not just with the teacher, but also with other students. Group discussion fosters student-to-student interaction and builds relationships. Students share their knowledge with others and offer their previous experiences. A synergy is created from a pooling of resources. Group discussion emphasizes learning, not teaching, and the teacher is not viewed as the authority, but as a guide.

ADVANTAGES OF GROUP DISCUSSION

Keeping warm was the original advantage of group discussion! Students were grouped in a circle around the wood burning stove in the one room school house, and discussion ensued. Group discussion presents a number of modern day advantages as a teaching method.

1. Compared to one-to-one tutoring, the small group is more economical in the use of resources.
2. The facilitator of the group knows members and can clarify each person's level of existing knowledge.
3. The group can help select topics, issues, and content for discussion.
4. Synergy of group members usually produces a better end result than individuals pursuing a goal alone.
5. Group discussion develops skill in speech, leadership, listening, and self-confidence.
6. Group discussion activities develop responsibility and discipline.
7. Group discussion facilitates problem-solving.
8. Groups stimulate thought and create a sense of discovery.
9. Group members learn to respect the ideas and attitudes of others.
10. Relationships are encouraged which contribute to personal growth and understanding.
11. Students share experiences and knowledge.
12. Group discussion fosters student-to-student interaction.
13. Group discussion motivates students for further learning.
14. Groups prepare students for future life whereby they will function as members of many groups.

Group Discussions do not all look alike. Different goals influence a range of the learning environment, the style of the facilitator, and the task of the group as depicted below.

Characteristics of Learning Environment Continuum

Hard	Soft
Think	Feel
Build Skills	Understand
Information	Ideas
Solve Problems	Share experiences
Product centered	Process focused

Facilitator Style Continuum

Strict	Relaxed
Controlling	Permissive
Dominating	Participative
Director	Guide
Manipulate	Stimulate
Dull	Enthusiastic
Muddled	Organized

Group Goal

Social	Task

Not every group starts out strong. Groups go through a process of evolution, gaining experience each time they are together. Groups have also been described as going through these five stages:

Forming -	get to know one another
Storming -	feel uncomfortable and frustrated
Norming -	group members establish norms or rules
Performing -	function well, understand roles and responsibilities, and task
So Longing -	groups complete task and prepare to move on

SUCCESSFUL GROUP LEARNING

If group discussion is unfamiliar, you may wonder how you will evaluate its effectiveness. Look for the following elements as a guide:

1. Students have an opportunity to talk and express freely.
2. Students have a sense they created something.
3. Students feel comfortable and participate actively.
4. Students feel their efforts are encouraged and supported.
5. Students are clear on the purpose and have a sense of commonality of goal mutual interest.
6. Students appreciate good facilitation.
7. Students come prepared and are cooperative during discussion.

These elements can be achieved when:

1. Group members understand, respect, and accept each other.
2. Members share some common identity.
3. Communication is open and honest.
4. Topic and content is meaningful.
5. Members collaborate for group good.
6. Students feel free to confront problems.
7. Students are clear on the decision making process.
8. Group members agree on ground rules governing discussion.
9. Students are informed of the outcome.

Group discussion alters the traditional role of both the teacher, referred to as the facilitator, and the students. Clarifying roles and responsibilities reduces the level of ambiguity and uncertainty.

TEACHER AS FACILITATOR

The word facilitator comes from "facil" - to make easy. Remembering this is helpful when becoming familiar with the new role.

1. Facilitator sets the climate so members are physically and psychologically comfortable and not threaten. Chairs arranged in a

circle allow for good eye contact with all members. The facilitator sits as part of the group and does not stand as an authority figure. It is also a good idea to rotate seats with other group members to diminish the idea of the "teacher chair." Traditionally, this is the chair at the head of the table, so avoid that one.

2. The facilitator strives for a balance, not necessarily 50/50, of focusing the group on both the process of group discussion as well as the product or outcome.
3. Guidance is provided in a supportive, non-direct way.
4. The facilitator is in a position to diagnose needs of the members and to determine their level of competence in an area.
5. Participation by all group members is encouraged through probing by the facilitator.
6. The facilitator is available as a resource.
7. The facilitator ensures evaluation occurs, and solicits group member input.
8. Generally, the facilitator keeps the discussion focused on the topic and moving toward the goal, however this role can become a student role.

The facilitator's role changes as students progress and the group develops. Initially, the facilitator attempts to model group behavior. The facilitator models the thinking process for students by using questions to solve problems.

The facilitator follows modeling with coaching. He or she interjects occasional guidelines if needed, and challenges the students only if they wander, miss important objectives, or act confused.

Finally, a good facilitator works toward the stage of fading into the background. Students demonstrate they are capable of functioning on their own by taking responsibility for the group's and their own learning. The educational responsibilities of the students in small group learning is far greater than in other teaching/learning methods.

STUDENT ROLES AND RESPONSIBILITIES

1. Students come prepared for discussion and fulfill responsibilities assigned.

2. Group members admit knowledge deficiencies, ask for help, and learn how to remedy weak areas.
3. Students participate in discussion in open, honest way.
4. Students give and accept criticism and challenge each others' thinking.
5. Group members respect each others' opinions and viewpoints.
6. Students are flexible and open to new experiences.
7. Students exercise courtesy and follow ground rules.
8. Group members offer feedback and evaluate themselves and others.
9. Group members take on different roles.
10. Students develop the attitude that each person is important to the group achieving its goals.

Xvxn though my typxwritxr is an old modxl, it works quitx wxll xxcxpt for onx of thx kxys. I'vx wishxd many timxs that it workxd pxrfxctly. Trux, thxrx arx forty two kxys functioning wxll xnough, but just onx kxy not working makxs thx diffxrxncx. Somxtimxs, it sxxms to mx that our group is somxwhat likx my typxwritxr -- not all thx kxy pxoplx arx working propxrly. You may say, "Wxll, I'm only onx pxrson. It won't makx much diffxrxncs." But you sxx, thx group, to bx xffxctivx, nxxds thx activx participation of xvxry pxrson. Thx nxxt timx you think your xfforts arxn't nxxdxd, rxmxmbxr my typxwritxr, and say to yoursxlf: "I am a kxy pxrson and nxxdxd vxry much."

Unknown

ANTICIPATING POTENTIAL PROBLEMS

As a facilitator, be alert to potential problem areas. If prepared, you can effectively deal with the following situations.

MONOPOLIZING GROUP MEMBER

Avoid eye contact with the excessive talker. Move to position yourself near him or her; this will often silence the person. Thank the member for his/her contribution and suggest the group needs to hear from others. Try this technique: Each member of group is given five paper clips, M & Ms, or pennies. Each time individuals speak, one item is placed in the center.

When they run out of items, they cannot speak until everyone has placed all their items in the center of the table.

SILENT MEMBER

Engage the member by asking an "easy" question, or asking him or her to give an opinion because there are no right or wrong remarks.

Open the topic for discussion by allowing all members two minutes to state their views.

Engage the member as early as possible because the more time goes on, the more difficult it is to enter a discussion and the student becomes reluctant and withdraws even further.

Have members contribute in a small group first. Pair members with another member and have a brief discussion. This activity usually makes it less threatening to report back to the group at large.

State, "Let's hear from those who haven't had a chance to speak yet."

Remind group members of their responsibility to participate. Agree with them if the issue is raised that just because they are not verbalizing is not an indication they do not understand the topic. However, they are missing an opportunity to share the information with others and to receive feedback on their knowledge.

DISRUPTIVE MEMBER

These students may be "clowning" or having side conversations. Check out the reason for this behavior in a nonthreatening way. Involve them by assigning a task such as recorder or time keeper. Ask that the side discussion be shared for the benefit of the entire group. Pause in silence and see if this quiets the offenders. If the problem persists, rearrange the seating. Another tactic is to take a break, and talk privately with the students. If there are too many side conversations, this may be a red flag for the facilitator that the group is off track and needs remediation.

SLEEPERS

Keep in mind that "Every closed eye is not sleeping and every open eye is not seeing (or listening or learning!). Check it out.

LACK OF FOCUS

If the discussion is off track, rambling, or lack of movement is detected, the group may be unclear about their purpose and needs to be redirected. You can also ask students to keep comments related to the goal.

IRRELEVANT COMMENTS

If a group member makes a contribution that seems to come from left field, ask, "How is that related to the topic being discussed?"

If comments are made that suggests faulty thinking to you, ask, "How did you arrive at that comment?" Gaining insight into the thinking may make comments clearer. Often members who ask irrelevant questions or make statements are looking for some kind of acknowledgement. Control this behavior be giving the group member some positive reinforcement, or a task to perform such as recording the group or writing on the blackboard.

DEPENDENCY ON FACILITATOR

Remind students you are the guide on the side and vow not to dominate. Have a group member lead the discussion. Resist answering questions.

LAGGING DISCUSSION

This may signal it is time for a review or summary. Ask, "Where do we go from here?" Another question, "What additional information do you need to understand this point, issue, idea, or problem?"

The material may not be appropriate for the level of the group. Groups do have different educational levels and intellectual abilities. Groups need to plan the discussion in keeping with the potentiality of the group.

HOSTILE GROUP

This must be confronted. Open discussion and resolution is possible. Ask, "Why do you feel so strongly about this?" Or, "What troubles you about this?"

ARRIVE LATE

Start the group on time for those who are able to demonstrate responsible behavior. Have a private talk with late arrivals. Let everyone know the consequences of arriving late. Generally, deductions are made in participation points. Refer to end of chapter.

Rod Irwin, Ohio State University College of Medicine (Curry, 1991) describes the role of a facilitator this way:

> "There's nothing to it! Just sit up straight, smile
> a lot, nod occasionally, and keep your mouth shut."

TRAINING AS A FACILITATOR

Start by having group members state how they think they could be trained as a facilitator. This will generate responses such as reading, observing other groups either live or on videotape, taking part in systematic training from an experienced facilitator, and by a process of trial-and-error.

For a systematic process, make the training activity simulate that of a real group getting together for the first time. There are five major areas to cover in the training. They are Introductions, Climate Setting, Roles and Responsibilities, Objectives, and Evaluation.

Start the group with introductions. According to Schlesinger (1992) introductions serve at least seven purposes called The Seven C's. They are:

Climate setting to set the tone, get to know one another, and feel safe.
Commonalities identify like interests, experiences, or values.
Cohesion exercises to establish norms, trust, and develop a sense of a group rather than an individual.

Connecting activities provide a transition between sessions and topics.
Challenging activities are those that energize, expand, and stimulate.
Creative exercises provide brain teasers to help see another perspective
and uncover originality.
Closing activities are often overlooked, but are essential to acknowledge
group member's contributions, evaluate the learning, and finalize the
task.

Several creative ideas for accomplishing introductions are included at
the end of this chapter. One example is to have group members pair up
with someone in the room they know do not know very well. If members
find their own partners, the theory of sociometry comes into play. That
is, participants who have choosen for themselves show an improvement in
responses and performance. Recall the time when you went away from
home to camp, and experienced much more fun if you choose your own
bunk mate. Tell group they have five minutes to explore three ways they
are alike, and three ways they are different, and then be prepared to share
results with entire group. Maybe they both drive blue cars or spent their
summer vacations in the Rockies. As a facilitator, you want to participate
as a group member, so pair up with another person. Make it a three some if
necessary. Try to avoid having students simply state their names as an
introduction tactic. This is not very memorable. Use this time to explore
what previous knowledge and experience members bring to the group as
well. The goal for introductions is to allow group members to become
comfortable speaking and sharing information.

Climate setting is designed to encourage responsive behavior even
more. Ask the group to brainstorm as many advantages of group learning
as they can. Have a volunteer record the ideas on the board or a flip chart.
After all ideas are exhausted, I show a 10 minute video clip of an actual
group of students who go through this exercise the first time the group
meets. Compare the responses. Most often they are very similar.

Suggest to the group that in order for them to be as successful as
possible, certain personal characteristics are needed. You can use some
creative image here: tell group they are building a bridge across water, and
each characteristic makes a strong plank to the other side, or they are
constructing a chain, and each characteristic forms a link to complete a
strong chain. If the group has difficulty getting started, suggest honesty,
humor, punctuality, responsibility, or focus as desirable traits.

Briefly discuss that group discussion is a teaching/learning format that requires taking on new roles for the teacher and student, and a shift in responsibilities for both. For a point of reference, have the group respond to, "What does the teacher do as a facilitator that is different than a lecturer?" When that area is completed, have group respond to, "What roles and responsibilities do students take on that transform them into active learners?" Students volunteer for the roles needed for the session. For example, a time keeper, a recorder, and an encourager.

At this point, review with the group what has been accomplished. They have conducted introductions, first in a nonthreatening self selected pair, and then with the larger group. The process of climate setting began with an understanding of the advantages of using group discussion as a teaching/learning format which will motivate them. They also have identified characteristics group members bring to the group setting to make their unit function as effectively as possible. Recognizing that new roles and responsibilities are necessary, they have determined how the balance shifts to a shared partnership.

The foundations for the group have been set and the group is ready to move on to establish their purpose. **Objectives** are determined at this time. If a case is presented, the intended outcomes are delineated. Objectives keep the group task focused and guide the discussion.

Allow adequate time near the end to engage the group in their responsibility of **evaluation**. Groups evaluate their learning by determining if the objectives were achieved. They also evaluate their own performance and that of the facilitator. They can also critique each group member. This may be uncomfortable at first. Encourage each person to verbally state one thing the person next to him or her did well during the session, and one thing that could be improved next time. To evaluate self, students can assign a number from 1-20 and justify why they deserve the number. Students can determine what constitutes the range of points. For example:

    20 content/and or process leader
    18 contributes significantly
    16 contributes with some interaction
    14 occasional contributor

12 assumes a task
10 mostly silent
8 arrived late or left early - good interaction
6 arrived late or left early
5 both arrived late and left early
4 combination of arrives late/leaves early and silent
2 heartbeat

Students can determine criteria for participation. Objective criteria are listed on page 162. Additional formats for evaluation are included at the end of this chapter.

Conclude this segment by reminding members about the various opportunities they have to acquire skills in facilitating. There are numerous books on the subject. Videotape ongoing groups, and have those available for members to review. Tell them to be aware of what the facilitator does and what the students are doing while they watch. What was effective, what could be done differently? Notice problem areas and decide how they can handle them. Being a member of a group is good practice also. Once teachers are facilitating actual sessions, have a colleague observe them, through a two-way mirror if possible, or on videotape, or by sitting in the group as a silent observer. Assure them that experience can be a good teacher, and the more they facilitate and review the process, the more comfortable, confident, and competent they will become.

Ask the group what issues concern them about group discussion. Use their responses as a springboard for problem-solving. Use the information provided in this chapter on how to deal with potential problems.

If the group is available for serial training in facilitation skills, this next activity described is ideal for a follow-up session. Have a simulated group of students assembled. Give them an assigned role to play: hostile member, quiet member, disruptive member, and teacher-dependent member. Index cards can be provided for the simulated students.

Hostile Student: Maintain a very negative attitude. Speak with a hostile tone, "Why do we have to do this?" "Why do I have to be here?" "What does this have to do with biology?"

Nonparticipant: Be very reluctant to speak, appear to withdraw from the group. If asked a question, say, "I don't know." Appear to be sleeping at times.

Disruptive: Attempt "clowning" behavior. Bother the person next to you, get up and walk around, look out the window, read the newspaper.

Teacher-dependent: Rely on the teacher. Insist only the teacher has the right answers. Say, "Just tell us what to do."
Tell each member of the training group they will have approximately ten minutes to practice their skills in one of the following areas: introductions, climate setting to include advantages of group learning and characteristics group members bring to successful groups, roles and responsibilities for students and facilitator, determining objectives, and evaluating the group.
At the end of each ten minute time segment, have all group members critique what they observed.
At the start of training, I provide group members with a Facilitator Guide (Quam, 1992). This guide functions as an outline for the training, and allows group members to record key information. It can be reviewed at a later time when facilitators feel a need for review, reinforcement, or remediation. The guide is a source for activities used for groups also.

"Always remember what you have learned. Your education is your life, guard it well."

Proverbs 4:13

FACILITATOR EVALUATION

Please mark an "X" on each scale below to rate your response.

_____/
Interested in students   Uninterested

_____/
Encourages participation   Dominates discussion

_____/
Sets positive climate   Uncomfortable

_____/
Guides discussion   Non-directive

_____/
Enthuastic   Dull

_____/
Fair and impartial   Biased

_____/
Asks open questions   Asks closed questions

_____/
Builds relationships   Ignores learners

_____/
Flexible   Rigid

EVALUATION

Please mark an "X" on each scale below to rate your response of our small group.

_____/
Well organized   Muddled

_____/
Focused, good progression   Little progress

_____/
Cooperative   Competitive

_____/
Uses time constructively   Wastes time

_____/
Balanced participation   Uneven

_____/
Clear on objectives   Fuzzy on purpose

_____/
Shows respect   Disrespectful

_____/
Nonthreatening environment   Uncomfortable

_____/
Rotates tasks   Same old, same old

_____/
Students are prepared   Lack preparation

IDEAS FOR CONDUCTING INTRODUCTIONS IN GROUPS

The goal is for group members to get to know one another, and to establish a friendly, supportive learning environment where learners respect and trust one another. These exercises are low risk forms of disclosure. The key to successful introductions is to gear the activity toward the interests of the group, encourage sharing, make everyone feel accepted, and to have fun.

1. Ask group members to form dyads. Each person interviews the other. After a few minutes, they switch roles. Each person introduces the other to the entire group. Offer a few guidelines if needed: name, hometown, favorite book, favorite movie, etc.

2. Find a partner and work in pairs to identify four things you have in common (alike) and four things/ways you are different. After discovering these, each person reports two or three ways to the entire group. This helps establish the idea that groups are diverse and have varied experiences to bring to the group.

3. Have students list groups they have been part of for the past five years. Present information to entire group noting if group is more social or task oriented, and were experiences positive or negative, and what made them that way.

4. Each group member needs a sheet of paper and a pencil or pen. Everyone write a name on the top of the page. That is the WHO of a sentence. The paper is folded over and passed to the student on the right. That student adds an action which is the WHAT. Paper is again folded and passed to the right and the WHERE and WHEN are added. The final person adds the WHY, and folds the paper. All papers are placed in the center of the group and each person selects one. Students take turns reading the completed sentences out loud. This should generate some laughs and make the group relaxed and at ease.

5. Have available a roll of toilet paper. Pass it around the group and tell each group member to tear off a piece. The pieces can be any length they determine. When everyone has a length, announce that they will introduce themselves, giving as many facts as sections of toilet paper they tore off. Those who took a little, say a little, and those who took a lot, say more!

6. Ask group members to stand and form a circle. State that you are going to state your name and toss a ball (tennis, nerf) to a person across the circle. That person states his or her name and repeats your name, and tosses the ball to a third person who repeats the names and action. This continues until everyone catches the ball and has an opportunity to repeat the entire list of names.

7. Have members form pairs, exchange names, and share, "What I expect to get from this group and what I can contribute."

8. In advance, write each word from the list of sentences below on an index card. Capitalize the first letter of the first word in each sentence only. Give each person in the group four cards, making certain they are mixed and do not form a sentence. Instructions to the group members are that they are to use only four cards to form a sentence and that they have 10 minutes to do it. No other instructions are given. If the group asks you, it is OK to switch and trade cards, which is the only way they will be able to form sentences.

The value of this exercise is to demonstrate how groups can work together to in order to complete any exercise and to do it efficiently.

It looks like snow.	The flowers are blooming.
Birds are singing sweetly.	My uncle goes fishing.
The doctor seems caring.	The patients are recovering.
The moon is yellow.	The spotted dog barks.
I really like teaching.	The bees are buzzing.

Use the same number of sentences as there are group members. Several combinations are possible. However, group members must collaborate so everyone has a sentence. This means a member may form a sentence, but later need to trade cards in order for all members to have a sentence. Example: I really like teaching could also be: I really like fishing, I really like snow, or I really like flowers.

PARTICIPATION CRITERIA

1. Displays respect for other group members.
2. Identifies with group culture.
3. Displays commitment to the group activities.
4. Participates fully in group activities. Volunteers for tasks.
5. Contributes new ideas to the discussion.
6. Acts receptive to the ideas of other members.
7. Promotes the use of creative thinking in the group.
8. Evaluates ideas using critical thinking skills.
9. Provides feedback to group members.
10. Communicates effectively with all group members.
11. Uses active listening during discussions.
12. Works with other members to achieve consensus decisions.
13. Helps keep the group focused on objectives and tasks.
14. Accepts the authority of the designated leader.
15. Displays knowledge and willingly shares it. Acknowledges ways of gathering information.
16. Adheres to group norms.
17. Cooperates with group members to achieve objectives.

LESSON PLAN

Goal - To acquire knowledge of the role of facilitator and to gain skills in using group discussion as a teaching methodology.

Objectives:
To discuss the dynamics of group process.
To compile a list of learning advantages of group discussion.
To identify roles and responsibilities of teacher and student.
To name elements of a successful group discussion.
To list group roles and functions.

Pre-Opening:
Have group members use the "broken word" game to form sentences.

I. Introduction
Ask participants what groups they have been part of previously.
Brainstorm advantages of group learning. (Reflecting on previous group involvement will elicit advantages).

II. Body
How can groups be formed? (number off, random, alphabetically, each person receives a playing card-all those with hearts form one group, clubs another, etc.)
Review group discussion continuums.
Discuss roles and responsibilities of teacher and students.
Name potential problems. Form groups and discuss ways of handling the problems. Share remarks.
Present the following situations. Individuals can respond indicating how they would handle the situations, or small groups can be formed and the situations discussed.
Situation 1. You have just introduced the topic for the discussion with an excellent provocative question and there is silence. What do you do?

Situation 2. One student says, "I don't understand where this
discussion is leading. Why don't you just tell us what you want us to
know?" What do you do?

Situation 3. There are two students in the group who have not said
anything since the discussion started. Their expressions indicate
displeasure. What do you do?

When reporting responses, have group indicate if their response focused
on process over content, individual need over group needs, and student
responsibility over facilitator role.

III. Conclusion

Why is acquiring the necessary skills for facilitating a group discussion
difficult?

Have each person contribute a key point from this session.

Resources: Broken Word Game

WORKSHEET

How can groups be formed?

When starting a new group, how can introductions be handled?

What important elements are included in setting the climate for group learning?

What characteristics do group members contribute to make a group successful?

What is the role of the facilitator?

What are the students' responsibilities?

What roles do students perform in groups?

How are objectives determine in group discussions?

What criteria is used to determine group member's participation?

What forms of evaluation are used for groups?

Chapter 9

WHAT IF LECTURES ARE OUTLAWED?

"Education is not the filling of a pail; it is the lighting of a fire."

-William Butler Yeats

The lecture persists as the most commonly used methodology in teaching. One reason it is used so frequently is because teachers model the way they were taught. Also, they are comfortable with it because it is familiar. Some have a sense that lecturing is just like talking, therefore few skills are needed. A strong case can be made that lecturing involves less preparation time. This may not be true initially, but everyone can cite a teacher who simply dusted off the yellowed copy of his or her notes, rarely updating or incorporating any new ideas before entering the classroom. And some teachers use the lecture format because it is authoritarian and a means to dominate and establish control. But I believe most often it is consistently used because teachers do not have the skills to confidently use any other methods. If this is holding you back, this book can acquaint and equip you with numerous alternatives.

Originally it was necessary to lecture, a Latin word "lagere" which means to read, because there were few books. Often the teacher was the only one with a book, and therefore, read the information to the students. This made sense at the time.

Some relief from the dominance of the lecture came when printing presses were invented allowing for wider circulation of books. But lead pencils were scarce, so still the lecture persevered.

Even though the lecture remains an old standby, major drawbacks to lecturing are:

> it is authoritarian
> it is a one-way form of communication
> it has not been determined to be the best way to teach
> students are passive
> it appeals most to auditory learners
> little visual support is provided
> 80% of what is heard in a lecture is lost in eight weeks
> the relationship element in the teaching/learning process is diminished

WHEN ARE LECTURES APPROPRIATE?

The lecture method can still be used when appropriate. That is, when placed within a context that considers the specific objectives of the session, the complexity of the subject or content, the physical environment of the room, the abilities of the learners including learning styles, and the amount of time available to deliver the essential content.

Advantages of using the lecture method include the economy of student to teacher ratio. Imagine the difficulty of providing tutors for 200 students for a one-on-one teaching experience. Lectures can be used by experts who have synthesized large amounts of information. New material including recent developments not yet available in print are often delivered by lectures. The lecture is a good method for conveying factual information, but stay away from values and beliefs. These topics are better suited to group discussion. Teaching is more than transmitting information. It is a human transaction, otherwise teachers would be eliminated and students would rely totally on tapes and computers.

A large room full of people does not automatically suggest that a lecture is the method of choice, but a large space can deter even the most determined active learning advocate. Distance makes interaction more difficult. Eye contact is diminished, and the sound of the voice is different, even with a front of the room. Students are not seen individually, but remain faces in the crowd.

Large numbers of students can inhibit some students from participating because the risk is greater. Students hate to make a mistake or ask a silly question, and to do so and risk the ridicule of 100 students is simply too great a risk. So, they remain silent, fading into the sea of anonymity.

Physically, if the seats are anchored to the floor rendering them unmovable, discussions in small groups are nearly impossible to orchestra. This encourages students to remain passive spectators, looking for the front of the room seeking to be entertained.

HOW TO MAKE LECTURES EFFECTIVE

Acting as an advocate of active learning does not mean forsaking the lecture. It does mean altering the more traditional lecture format to include more responsibility, more variety, and more action on the part of the students.

1. Pause at least three times in an hour long class session to allow brief interludes for the students to turn to the next person, and clarify and/or assimilate course content.
2. Use frequent short writing exercises. Ask students to write a short summary of the previous lecture. Ask a few to read aloud and invite class members to respond.

   Give students a chance to practice their understanding of the material by writing a short piece.

   At the end of class ask students to develop 2-3 questions about the material. Ask students to note 1-2 applications of the content. Ask students to solve a problem or make a decision relative to the content of the session.

3. Halfway through the session, have students work in pairs to discuss questions you distribute to them, or use the questions from item 2, point 3 above.

4. Have students put their pens down and listen after you present the learning objectives for the session. Half way through the session, have them write down in outline form, what they recall. Expand from there, time permitting, and have the students form groups of 4-5 and add to their individual outlines. This group interaction is cooperative and the notes produced are usually superior.
5. Be responsive to students. Occasionally, devote the class session to student questions, issues, or concerns. Solicit ideas and have the class rank them in order. This list in order of importance becomes the outline for the session. (Bonwell, 1991).
6. Clearly introduce the topic and key objectives of the lecture at the beginning. Include frequent summaries. Or, stop periodically and allow students to work in pairs to summarize the material presented. Then have selected pairs report to the group at large.
7. Supplement with visuals. The chalkboard is good if all students can see it. Write legibly and large and be sure the chalkboard is well lighted. Technical terms and important vocabulary need to be displayed for students by using a flip chart, overhead transparencies, the chalkboard, or handouts.
8. Use concrete examples and analogies so students can conceptualize concepts within a familiar framework. Have students individually, then in pairs, give examples of concepts presented. Students can also volunteer examples from their own experiences.
9. Build in some redundancy using repetition, expansions and paraphrases.
10. Aim for students to apply the knowledge presented. Build in time for students to develop situations where concepts can be used.
11. Stimulate thinking by stopping the lecture and asking students to predict what could happen in a situation, given certain principles or concepts. Pose a real problem and have students engage in a problem solving exercise.
12. For transition from the auditory style of a lecture to the visual learning style of students, have students create flow charts, graphs, or tables of the information presented.

Understanding when to use the lecture as a teaching method is a positive step in delivering information effectively using the lecture format. There is a time and a place for lectures, and using the ideas presented in this chapter enhance the presentation so it utilizes some principles of student participation. The ideas stated here can all be incorporated to create more vibrant lectures. Most require a change and change is never easy.

"If you want truly to understand something, try to change it."

- Kurt Lewin

LESSON PLAN

Goal - To create ways of using the lecture format as a more effective teaching method.

Objectives:

To explain advantages of the lecture teaching method.
To identify ways to overcome disadvantages of the lecture teaching method.
To apply strategies that support an oral presentation.
To consider ways to expand the student's role from passive to active.

Pre-Opening:
Demonstrate the origin of lecture (to read). Indicate that long ago printing presses and pencils were invented. Pose the question, "So why has the lecture persevered?"

I. Introduction
After a brief review of the history of the lecture, move into determining when to use the lecture as a teaching method, and how to make it effective.

II. Body
What would indicate that a lecture is effective?
2 way communication
students become active
support materials used (AV, props)

Ask participants to discuss why they use lectures and to name situations where lectures offer distinct advantages
Share ways to overcome or reduce disadvantages of lecturing
Brainstorm additional strategies for students to become active learners

III. Conclusion

Review

Resources:

WORKSHEET

Why does the lecture persist?

When should the lecture format be used?

What does an effective lecture look like?

What can you incorporate into a lecture to make it effective?

Chapter 10

SOCRATIC METHOD

"We use the Socratic method. I call on you. I ask you questions. You answer. Through my questions you learn to teach yourself. This develops in you the ability to analyze facts. My questions spin the tumblers of your mind. We do brain surgery. You teach yourself the law and I train your mind. You come in with a skull full of mush, and you leave thinking like a lawyer."

- Professor Kingfield in *The Paper Chase.*

Lectures have a long standing history and remain popular today with some reports stating teachers do 80% of the talking in the classrooms. However, using questions as a teaching format was also established centuries ago, and is one way to reduce teacher talk time.

Socrates was a teacher whose style was so effective that a teaching method was named after him. In his teaching, Socrates held the belief that students possessed knowledge innately. It was his role as teacher, to pose questions that would stimulate the student's thinking, thereby drawing previously untapped knowledge out of the student's head.

The Socratic method is directly opposite the authoritarian method which is premised on the belief that it is the teacher who has all the knowledge. It is the teacher's role to give it to the student. The contrast in these two methods is that the Socratic method focuses on stimulating the thought process, and the authoritarian lecture method focuses on conveying content or information.

Socratic questions help students explore their beliefs. The skills students learn in the thinking and reasoning process are complimentary to problem-solving. This method promotes a collaborative experience with an emphasis on helping students discover answers themselves. It is an active learning environment where both teacher and student participate.

"Students learn by becoming involved."

- Alexander Astin

Teachers may challenge the idea that they do not incorporate questions into their lectures. They may not realize that frequently when they pose a question, they answer it themselves. Often questions are ambiguous or rhetorical which sends a mixed message to students. On average, teachers ask a question and wait one second for an answer before providing the answer themselves.

It is more effective to use probing questions that require students to think, reason, and evaluate, rather than factual questions where students memorize the correct answers. However, 90% of the questions teachers do ask require factual recall.

TYPES OF QUESTIONS

Questions are classified by the range of responses and the level of thinking required. Two major classifications exist. They are:

CLOSED - limited thought, single word answer, answered quickly

a. memory (recall) good for review - not for testing understanding of student.

b. convergent - translate, interpret answer in own words used to further develop concepts.

OPEN - problem-solving, complex thinking required

a.   process - develop critical thinking, scientific method
b.   evaluation - opinion and judgment - student can take any position he/she can defend.

Bloom's (1956) taxonomy of questions is broader but also uses levels of thinking. It is:

1. Knowledge - who, what, recall, rote memory
2. Comprehension - describe, explain, interpret, translate into new form
3. Application - use facts to solve problems, relationships, apply rules or principles
4. Analysis - separate into component parts
5. Synthesis - put together to create new whole, variety of answers for a problem, uses imaginative and creative thinking
6. Evaluation - develop opinions, judgments; make decisions

WHY USE QUESTIONS?

Questions should reflect a definite purpose. Questions are used as a stimulus for interaction between the teacher and learner, and between learner and learner. Here are a dozen ways to promote interaction.

1. Diagnose students baseline knowledge level
2. Verify understanding, check comprehension, clarify what was said
3. Allow learners an opportunity to think creatively
4. Review content and assess readiness to continue
5. Stimulate discussion and increase learner participation
6. Establish a focus
7. Motivate learners
8. Vary the cognitive level
9. Probe beyond the initial thought, use questions as an extension of topic, or shift discussion to another level
10. Redirect
11. Involve everyone, keep students alert
12. Debate - Agree/disagree - Devil's advocate

HOW NOT TO USE QUESTIONS

Students react negatively to the Socratic teaching method if questions are used inappropriately. Do not use questions as a way of:

a reprimand

filling time

putting people on the spot

asking for too much data

posing obvious questions

asking ambiguous questions that confuse

asking yes and no questions which usually lead to a follow-up "why" question

asking "why" questions which make students defensive. Use "how" whenever possible

calling attention to better students

looking for a right and wrong answer only

When teachers are reluctant to use questions as a teaching format, some of the reasons may be related to:

1. Inexperience
2. Control
3. Time
4. Need to cover all the content
5. Want to appear knowledgeable
6. They get little or no response

You condition your students early not to respond by using rhetorical questions, or answering your own questions. A typical teacher waits only one second for an answer. The strategy is to wait longer. The longer you wait, the longer the student's answer will be. Teachers need to give students time to think, which is the ultimate goal of using the questioning technique.

THE CHRONICLE OF HIGHER EDUCATION

EFFECTIVE USE OF QUESTIONS

Hints for asking questions include:

1. Ask question and wait 3-5 seconds. Recite to yourself, "Baa, baa, black sheep, have you any wool? Yes sir, yes sir, three bags full." The time it takes for you to run through this ditty is about five seconds. And, by waiting longer, the learner's answer will also be longer-about three bags longer!
2. Call student by name or call on a specific student. Ask the student to state name before answering the questions. This will help you get to know the students.
3. Respond to wrong answer by saying "How did you arrive at that response?" Use this tactic when students answer correctly also.
4. Patterned turns reduce anxiety and is an efficient way to ensure that all students have equal opportunity to interact with the teacher. The tag team approach has one student answering a question and then "tagging" another student to answer the next question. Students are allowed to pass which helps reduce anxiety. Teachers can use the pattern of asking questions of all students wearing green one day, blue some other day. Of course you do not announce the color in advance.
5. React to students' questions without giving an evaluation.
6. Do not say, "That's a good question." That is your evaluation. If you need to say something, try, "I am glad you raised that."
7. If a student answers, "I don't know", rephrase the question or give an example for clarification. Simply repeating the question again is not sufficient to broaden the student's understanding and formulate an answer.
8. Plan questions when developing the lesson plan. Keep in mind that one isolated question does not have the power that a sequence of questions does. A synergy is created from the cumulative effect of asking a series of questions.
9. Questions should be concise and require a thoughtful response, not simply a quick recall.
10. Address questions to the entire group, then ask a specific person to respond. This allows all students an opportunity to formulate a response, not just the person called on.
11. Repeat student response to ensure everyone heard it, including you.

These phrases help you DEFLECT student questions rather than providing all the answers yourself.

"Bill, I'd like you to answer Ruth's question."
"Let's hear what other students have to say about that."
"Mary, what do you think about what John said?"
"Ann, what can you add?"
"Someone help Joe out."
"Jill, expand on Sue's comments."

In summary, using questions effectively helps students develop critical thinking skills. Questions can serve as 100% of the teaching method, or can be successfully used with other methods to increase student participation. Different types of questions are used depending on the situation, however, using open-ended questions is the most desirable to elicit information requiring thinking. To incorporate questions into the teaching/learning environment requires skill, just as using other teaching methods does. Your effort in using questions is rewarding. Questions are stimulating for both the teacher and the learners and can be viewed as a method for adding a positive dimension to the classroom.

"The reward for work well done is the opportunity to do more."

- Jonas Salk, M.D.

LESSON PLAN

Goal - To use questions as an effective teaching method as a stimulus for increasing interaction and participation.

Objectives:
To recognize types of questions.
To use questions for a variety of instructional purposes.
To formulate a repertoire of questioning skills.

Pre-Opening:
 Attention Getter: Cartoon "I sense a hand is raised, yet I can not turn around."
Has this happened to you? What other reasons do teachers have for not using questioning as a teaching method?

I. Introduction
 Today we will...
 This is important because...
 At the end of the session you will...

II. Body
 A. Types of Questions
Define and discuss open and closed questions.
Describe the six levels of questions based on Bloom's taxonomy.
How are these levels determined?
Activity: Provide sample questions and have group indicate which of the six levels is being used.
Provide information on how to phrase questions at the different levels.
For example:

Knowledge -	Who, what, when, where, or how questions
Comprehension -	How can you retell in your own words?
Application -	How is...an example of...?
	Why is...significant?
	How is...related to...?

Analysis -   What are the parts of...?
                  Who can list...?

Synthesis -   What ideas can you add to...?
                  What can you infer from...?
                  What might happen if you combine...?

Evaluation -   What do you think about...?
                  How would you prioritize...?
                  How did you make that decision about...?

B. How to use questions

Have group discuss the various purposes of using questions.

C. How NOT to use questions
D. Techniques for using questions effectively.
E. Provide handout on Asking the Right Questions

III. Conclusion

As a summary and throughout the session, MODEL various kinds of questions and techniques for properly incorporating questioning behaviors into your teaching.

Resources: Handout: "Asking the Right Questions"

ASKING THE RIGHT QUESTIONS

Questions Designed to Open Discussion

1. What do you think about the problem as stated?
2. What has been your experience in dealing with this problem?
3. Who can offer suggestions on facts we need to better our understanding of the problem?

Questions Designed To Broaden Participation

1. Now that we have heard from a number of our group members, I would like to hear the ideas of the others who have not added their ideas.
2. How do the ideas presented so far sound to those who have been thinking about them?
3. Who else can add information?

Questions Designed to Limit Participation

1. We appreciate your comments, and now we want to hear from some of the other members.
2. There have been several good statements; who else can make   some comments?
3. Please hold any additional comments until everyone has had an opportunity to speak.

Questions Designed to Focus Discussion

1. Where are we now in relation to our discussion goal?
2. Who can review what we have discussed?
3. What progress have we made in this discussion?
4. Those comments are interesting. How are they related to the situation we are discussing?

Questions Designed to Help Move the Group Along

1. Have we spent enough time on this section so we can move along?
2. Because of our limited time, could we look at the next issue?
3. If we have gone far enough on this issue, could we shift our attention to another area?

Adapted from: (Trecker and Trecker, 1952).

WORKSHEET

How are questions used in your teaching?

Develop questions in each of the six levels from a current lesson plan or training session.

Determine which techniques you want to use more often (i.e. deflecting questions, using questions to develop critical thinking, using open rather than closed questions, using questions to increase student participation).

What strategies will you use to incorporate questions into your teaching?

What did you learn about how NOT to use questions?

Chapter 11

PROBLEM-BASED LEARNING (PBL)

"Teachers are those who use themselves as bridges, over which they invite their students to cross; then having facilitated their crossing, joyfully, collapse, encouraging them to create bridges of their own." (Canfield and Hansen, 1996).

WHAT IS PBL?

An emerging trend in education in recent years has been characterized by relying less on the teacher as an authority and shifting the responsibility of learning to the students by engaging them in active learning. One of the most common methodologies is problem-based learning. The goal of this chapter is to introduce PBL, its philosophy and techniques.

Problem-based learning is defined using both a philosophical and a methodological context. In order to learn and successfully use the skills and techniques of PBL, the more abstract philosophical foundation upon which PBL is based must be embraced. This requires taking on some new attitudes; attitudes that often differ from those acquired through the traditional process of being socialized to education.

PBL is a philosophy that embraces the principle that students learn through a teacher-learner interaction that involves active participation by both! Active learning requires students to do more than passively listen while the teacher lectures. Chapter 4 presents an expanded version of active learning. Again, this is a shift from the more traditional model of education. Students are involved by "doing things" and by "thinking about what they are doing." Active learning fosters an environment where students are encouraged to mentally and/or physically participate in a variety of activities. For example, active students are reading, reflecting, writing and discussing, all of which are designed to require students to think, and to clarify their thinking.

> "Thinking is the hardest work there is, which is probably the reason so few engage in it."

- Henry Ford

The basic principle of PBL is to put learners in a group and give them a problem to solve. In medical education for example, the problem is "the patient", therefore, students are given a particular patient situation and confronted with the task as a source for learning. This challenge is arranged or "simulated" to be similar to what they will actually be confronted with in their professional futures. This educational process enables students to develop the required reasoning and critical thinking skills more efficiently than they would in the traditional method where the teacher provides the information and the student, relying on rote memorization, is tested on it. (Walton and Matthews, 1989).

PBL advocates stress that it is the only known method for preparing future professionals to be able to adapt to change, for learning how to reason critically, and also for attaining integrated cumulative learning. (Walton and Matthews, 1989).

Facts are remembered better if there is some effort involved in acquiring the information. Therefore, if teachers are willing to give students all the information, (even though that is not possible because of the information explosion experienced in recent years coupled with the half-life of information) then students exert little effort to discover the information on their own.

> "Telling is not teaching, and listening is not learning."

- Paul Baker

One way to promote student effort is for students to become self-directed learners. Self-directed learning involves students being able to assess their own needs, monitor their learning, determine the appropriate resources, apply what has been learned, and have input into the evaluation of the outcomes of their learning. Students assume progressively more responsibility for their education or the learning process as they gain skills needed to function in such a way. Specific skills include: responsibility, self-motivation, organizational ability, capacity for independent learning, ability to function in groups, and self-evaluation. Becoming self-directed is an internal change in thinking as much as it is the external process of management of the instruction.

If philosophy is thought of as "abstract", how then can PBL be viewed in a concrete way? Being familiar with the philosophical constructs of PBL provides a foundation that assists you in developing the skills and techniques associated with PBL. Skills include writing cases, facilitating group discussions, and redesigning curricula which will be discussed later.

Methodology

PBL is recognized as a broad term that utilizes a variety of teaching methods. PBL is frequently associated with group learning via group discussion around a case. However, a more comprehensive approach is to view PBL as an umbrella term that includes a wide spectrum of teaching methods. Any method is appropriate when it is consistent with the active learning approach. At the center of PBL is the group discussion, but PBL needs to be supported by other learning experiences such as: field trips, laboratory exercises, self-paced modules, simulations, computer-assisted instruction, independent reading and/or projects, hands-on skill activities, and large group discussions. Even lectures can be classified as PBL, if they are dynamic, thought provoking and incorporate exercises to allow students to actively participate. Refer to Chapter 9 on lectures.

"To ask faculty to change a curriculum is like asking someone to move a graveyard. It can be done, but it is a funky, messy, complicated, long process."

— Johnnetta Cole, in *Composing a Life* by Mary Catherine Bateson (Atlantic Monthly Press, 1989), p.97.

R.I.P.

Curriculum

PBL needs to be seen in a context broader than the methods used. It is part of a whole curricular approach, not merely a method in its own right.

There is less emphasis on transmitting information from the content expert (teacher) to the student using the lecture format. The teaching/learning process becomes student-centered, focusing on what the student is doing, not on what the teacher does.

HERMAN®

6-16   © 1977 Jim Unger

Distributed by United Media

"They don't give us time to learn anything in school; we have to listen to the teacher all day."

PBL curriculum promotes retention and application, not memorization. It is essential that evaluation methods reflect more application of knowledge and skills using hands-on exercises or demonstration of competencies.

Two important skills students learn are problem-solving and critical thinking. Students are involved and challenged by higher-order thinking such as analysis, synthesis, and evaluation, and less on the lower levels of knowledge and comprehension in Bloom's (1956) classification of cognitive skills typology.

ADVANTAGES

PBL, while not a panacea, does offer strategies that promote many of the new ideas that support how education is changing. Identified advantages over more traditional education are that PBL:

Develops Critical Thinking Skills
Requires Collaborative Learning Methods
Acknowledges Student Diversity
Acknowledges Student's Prior Learning and Experience
Develops Communication Skills and Interpersonal Skills
Equips Students for Lifelong Learning - Learning How To Learn
Develops Student's Sense of Responsibility
Uses Relevant Material and Encourages Application
Accesses and Uses Varied Resources
Fosters Teamwork
Promotes Positive Attitude About School
What follows is a further explanation of each advantage.

CRITICAL THINKING

Critical thinking is the ability to reason which requires thinking on the meta cognitive level. The goal for developing critical thinking skills in students is to enable them to make judgments in complex situations on the basis of sound reason, adequate evidence, and articulated values. It is akin to problem-solving, but different in that the "solutions" cannot be verified empirically, or based entirely on "data." Because solutions cannot be tested, their plausibility is held up by the supporting reasons offered. One way to develop critical thinking in students is to require students to use content in projects. This is most often achieved by using structured small group work in which students clarify concepts, explore complex problems, debate issues, and seek resources of both a human and material nature.

Kurfiss (1988) defines critical thinking as an investigation whose purpose is to explore a situation, phenomenon, question, or problem to arrive at a hypothesis or conclusion about it that integrates all available information and that can therefore be convincingly justified. All assumptions are open to question, divergent views are aggressively sought, and the inquiry is not biased in favor of a particular outcome. The outcomes of critical inquiry are twofold: a conclusion and the justification offered in support of it.

COLLABORATIVE LEARNING

To collaborate is to work together in a way that encourages exploring, discussing, and negotiating. It encompasses the concept of synergy, that is, the whole created through the efforts of many, is stronger than each individual piece created separately.

Collaborative Learning and Cooperative Learning definitions blur. Combining both definitions results in students working jointly with others in intellectual endeavors for mutual benefit.

To offer an example, the field of medicine relies on interdependence and consultation. PBL fosters this work and social dependency model. PBL groups are structured to imitate the "real world." Collaborative learning helps students remove the competitive element from their learning process. Quality circles in business and industry are a response to what education has learned about people working collaboratively.

STUDENT DIVERSITY

Nearly all higher education campuses are attuned to the changing student demographics evident over the last ten years. Previously the term "college student" conjured up an image of an 18 year old, white, male student. Campuses are now more reflective of society on a global level. As a result, students represent wide diversity in gender, age, geography, socio-economic, and ethnic backgrounds. In response, educators are attempting to become sensitive to the different learning needs these students articulate, and to move

away from the more traditional methods that may have been better suited to a
different species of student.

PRIOR LEARNING AND EXPERIENCE

Because there is more diversity in students, it is reasonable that their varied
backgrounds and lifestyles also yield a range of life experiences. Adults bring
these experiences in search of connecting the new knowledge or skill to their
already existing knowledge. The learning theory evident is that learning the
unfamiliar occurs by connecting it with the familiar. Students come equipped
with the foundation, and seek to build upon it. This pool of experience is
valuable to students who draw upon it as a resource to help the group progress
toward its goals.

COMMUNICATION SKILLS

Communicating involves both talking and listening. With the traditional
lecture method, the communication process is one-way, with the teacher doing
all the talking. One problem with that method is that the teacher receives
limited feedback and has little assurance that students are listening, much less
learning. Students need to have opportunities to ask questions for clarification,
and they need to respond to teacher-asked questions. This provides an
indication to the teacher that there is an understanding that goes beyond
simply hearing. In small group discussions, students are participating, both
speaking and listening. Students are posing questions, and providing
information to each other. There is an emphasis on student-to-student
interaction, rather than teacher-to-student. Eventually, even the student labeled
"quiet" will vocalize. This occurs when the environment is comfortable, the
student is secure, and when the action of peer pressure is put in motion.

LIFELONG LEARNING

Education is not a product, but rather a process that spans a life time. The
challenge is to equip students with the ability to learn about learning. They
need skills that will assist them in identifying what it is they need to learn,
steer them to appropriate resources for information, analyze the information,

make decisions after reviewing possible alternatives, and to determine the effectiveness or evaluate the results after application.

STUDENT SENSE OF RESPONSIBILITY

In PBL, particularly in small group discussion, the role of the student is active and as a result, students take more responsibility for the learning process. Students are responsible to participate in discussions in an open, honest way. This requires risk taking, and can leave students open to criticism. However, another responsibility is to give and accept criticism, and view it as challenging each other on what the basis is for statements made. This is consistent with critical thinking, which requires students to justify their thinking. Viewing this process as a challenge is less threatening than viewing it as a criticism. Students are responsible for respecting each other's viewpoint and to question in a nonthreatening manner. Another responsibility is to exercise courtesy. Students need to be responsible for admitting any knowledge deficiencies they have, and need to be able to ask for help and to learn to remedy the deficiencies. Students need to complete assignments in advance and come to the group prepared for the discussions. Students are also responsible for being flexible.

RELEVANT MATERIAL AND APPLICATION

Knowledge is not enough. There must be meaningful information. Knowledge becomes relevant when it is connected to reality. Students need a practical education. PBL helps students acquire knowledge that is usable and can be applied to solve problems. This is because the learning is done in a context that helps students organize the material in their memory banks, and in a way that is more easily retrieved when needed. Retention of the information is based on the students' sense of the informational value and meaning.

ACCESS AND USE APPROPRIATE RESOURCES

Students are able to determine what resources they need to assist them in solving the learning issues identified. By accessing the resources independently, they become self-directed in their learning efforts as well as gain the skills of gathering and analyzing data.

Technology available in libraries today is a valuable resource. PBL encourages students to use current literature to supplement textbooks, utilizing online searches. Experts are also sought with the caveat that they respond only to specific questions raised by the students.

TEAMWORK

Groups of students identify what work has to be done and each student volunteers to complete a part of the work. If a student does not follow through and bring back the information the next time the group meets, this has a profound affect on the total work the group is attempting to do. Peer pressure insures that each student develops the ability to function as a team member. This is a lifelong skill because in order to be a productive member of society, people are required to function on a team or as part of a group.

Students in groups often assume roles or task functions to help their group operate effectively. These tasks include: initiating, information seeking, information giving, clarifying or elaborating, summarizing, and consensus testing. Groups also have special emotional functions that are assumed by student members. These may include: encourager, harmonizer, compromiser, gate-keeper, or standard setter.

POSITIVE ATTITUDE ABOUT SCHOOL

"Education is serious business. If you're having fun, how could you possibly be learning anything?"

Michael Guillen, PhD.
Good Morning America
December 21, 1994

Learning can be fun! This is often a radical, foreign idea for most students who have been socialized to believe school is hard work and to enjoy school categorizes you as a "nerd" or "squid". Initially, students resist active learning and activities that encourage critical thinking because it is hard work.

One of the most common variables researched in PBL evaluation is the attitude of students participating in PBL. Studies have found that all students favor PBL to some degree. Some measurements used include: increased attendance, less student distress as indicated by depression, anxiety, and hostility. (Vernon and Blake, 1993). Questionnaires often ask students to report their feelings, and they are positive.

ISSUES

Having presented the advantages of PBL, let us now look at some of the issues to consider. Being aware of these issues can assist teachers in identifying potential problem areas and devising strategies to overcome or at least reduce them as they undertake a curricular revision or redesign to implement PBL.

Development of Cases
Case Content
Teacher Resistance
Student Resistance
Measurement of Outcomes
Content Expertise for Facilitators
Cost

DEVELOPMENT OF CASES

Authentic cases are preferred. These "paper" cases are written collaboratively and authored by a team representing content experts. Other faculty such as librarians, psychologists, and educators also contribute their expertise. Written cases are in book form, but computer formats also exist. One case can be used repeatedly. The emphasis shifts based on the objectives identified by the group. They determine the focus of a case and determine the expected outcomes.

At the initial group meeting of six to eight students and a facilitator, time is devoted to the process of establishing group dynamics. Laying the ground work for the process is essential and assists the group in accomplishing its task. Introductions are offered. Members discuss experiences they have had in other groups, facilitator elicits from students the advantages of group learning, ground rules for how the group will operate are established, roles and responsibilities as well as expectations are discussed. Students become familiar with how evaluation process will take place.

The objectives for the session are discussed after a brief case is presented.

The recorder puts categories on a board or flip chart. The categories are:

Facts Hypothesis Learning Issues

When questions are posed, probing questions are asked in response. Students then process the additional information. No information is provided unless it is specifically requested and justified.

Students bring resources to the session, but also identify additional resources that can be contacted before the next session. Lab results are given in as close to actual form as possible. In medical education, for example, actual EKG strips, x-rays, and CBC results are provided.

Students volunteer to further study the learning issues identified. Learning issues include a review of the already learned information, but focus on the acquisition and incorporation of new information. The facilitator ensures that the learning issues capture the intended case objectives. Students then leave the session and work independently to find answers by contacting resources. Students return to the group at a future date, usually a few days later and share information.

Additional questions are posed, additional learning issues may develop, and the case is moved to completion which is based on the earlier determined expected outcomes.

CASE CONTENT

Is it not equally important to teach students how to ask good questions, communicate effectively, critically analyze sources of information, research issues, draw on resources, reflect on consequences and appreciate diversity? (Meyers and Jones, 1993). The main goal of education is not the knowledge per se, but rather the ability of students to acquire a predisposition to learn.

It is the breathe of the material rather than the depth that can be an issue in PBL. Studies have been conducted to determine if students can identify the same objectives as faculty in PBL cases. Roughly 60% of the learning issues are uncovered by students.

TEACHER RESISTANCE

Introducing PBL into a curriculum is viewed as a change, both for teachers and students. Change can be both an opportunity or a danger. If viewed as "danger", resistance is the result. Fear of the unknown and a feeling of loss of control may intensify the resistance. Change can be presented as a constant, dynamic process that is "different" not good or bad. From this viewpoint, teachers can change when they have the new skills and knowledge and also the willingness or motivation to embrace the change. Of primary importance is good communication about the new roles and expectations.

Teachers are beginning to talk about teaching. Meyers and Jones (1993) characterize this as a change from the days when teachers surrounded their classrooms with psychological moats, and seldom discussed what went on within their castles.

Figure 8 : Teacher Resistance

STUDENT RESISTANCE

Most students are unfamiliar with PBL and need time to gain the skills necessary to succeed in PBL. Students tend to resist initially because PBL can be more difficult. The perceived difficulty is because of the responsibility students are given for the learning process, and because they are unfamiliar with PBL as an educational strategy where the teacher is not the authority figure, and because learning in a PBL environment may take more time.

Students seem to spend more time studying each week compared to the more traditional curriculum. The majority of students "like" learning in a PBL curriculum once they experience it.

MEASUREMENT OF OUTCOMES

On-going assessment and feedback are necessary. Short quizzes can be used to assess basic knowledge and understanding. Open-book exercises can be used to test how well students can apply problem-solving skills to actual cases. Modified essay questions are also used for evaluation purposes. A sample case consisting of one to two paragraphs that describe the problem can be given to students. Five or six short essay answers can be written by the student. These answers measure knowledge, comprehension, as well as application of the information.

Simulated situations can mimic real situations using controlled conditions. These are used successfully to observe if students can apply their knowledge and use the skills they acquire in a "staged" situation. Students demonstrate skills based on defined objectives as well as interpersonal skills. Competency is then determined.

CONTENT EXPERTISE OF FACILITATORS

Barrows (1988) suggests that process skills are more important than content expertise if you can have only one or the other. "...the ideal circumstance is for tutor to be expert both as a tutor and in the discipline being studied...the next best is teacher who is good at being a tutor." It is not acceptable to have a teacher who is an expert in the area of study, but a weak tutor. If the tutor is not an expert, the following things can be done to make him or her more comfortable:

1. have well-stated objectives
2. provide a set of learning issues
3. orient the tutor about each problem used. Identify their importance, why they were chosen, what the student should learn from them, and any particularly important points about traps or difficult issues that could arise
4. provide the tutor with an expert with whom he or she can consult.

Silver and Wilkerson (1991) showed that expert tutors tended to take a more directive role in the tutorials, spoke more often and for longer periods of time, provided more direct answers to students' questions, and suggested more items for discussion. There were also fewer student-to-student interactions. Students with less PBL experience tend to rely more on their tutor, therefore using facilitators with content expertise may be more helpful in the first year of a curriculum. Schmidt et al. (1993) determined that both subject-matter knowledge and process-facilitation skills seem to be necessary conditions for effective tutoring.

After one to two months, students enrolled in a PBL curriculum are so acculturated and so highly skilled in student-centered, self-directed learning that (1) they function independently of the facilitator at least 90% of the time, and (2) they rarely care what the facilitator's ideas are since they so highly value their own work according to Zeitz and Paul (1993).

COST

PBL results in increased utilization of the library. It is essential to have a library that can make available the resources sought independently by PBL students. The library's readiness to support PBL must be assessed. Five areas of assessment are advised by Rankin (1993):

1. Collection. It is recommended that there be a robust collection of books and journals in addition, non-print resources may also be required.

2. Library instruction program. Students will need skills to fully utilize the technology afforded in libraries to locate the resources they identify.
3. Facility. Some libraries have indicated a need to have additional audiovisual equipment and computer workstations.
4. Staffing. More library staff are required if students are encouraged to find resources independently, rather than from a suggested reading list.
5. Budget. This will depend on how many modifications result from the assessment of the first four items. Libraries may experience an increased use of photocopy machines.

Spaces are necessary where groups of six to eight students meet with their tutor without excess noise and other environmental interruptions. Traditional classrooms can be used if the seating is arranged in a circle to encourage good discussion and eye contact.

Equipment is very basic, and is limited to a place to write, such as a chalkboard, white board, or flip chart which are relatively inexpensive pieces of equipment.

Facilitators must be trained. Training focuses on guiding teachers to understand their new role as facilitators and to assist them in developing the skills necessary for that new role. Both skills and attitudes need to be addressed. A successful training program developed by Quam (1992) included five areas: introductions, climate setting, roles and responsibilities, objectives, and evaluation. The training consisted of a simulated group experience as well as a Facilitator Handbook. Teachers were encouraged to observe other experienced facilitators, view videotapes of groups, and to read *The Tutorial Process*. Chapter 8 provides additional information on facilitator training.

After the structured training, the following advice was given to launch the teachers in their new roles:

"For the things we have to learn to do before we do them, we learn by doing them."

-Aristotle

Cost increases with class size because the number of facilitators increases, unlike in traditional lecture classes where the teacher-student ratio is not impacted by size. PBL requires an investment in teacher training and development, although this is important in any teaching situation. Curriculum revision takes an extensive time commitment, especially in the early stages.

This chapter presented an overview of problem-based learning as an educational process. It included perspectives from both the philosophical and the methodological approaches. Advantages of using PBL were presented indicating that positive results can be attributed to PBL. Issues that have confronted some institutions attempting such a curricular shift were also revealed. Strategies for minimizing these were discussed.

In conclusion, PBL represents a positive shift for education. It addresses some of the major problems that have confronted the more traditional model of education. PBL relies less on the authoritarian teaching model and espouses rather a teacher/learner partnership with shared responsibilities. The focus is on student learning which is the ultimate goal of education. The learning is greater when there is active participation, relevant content, and application of skills or knowledge to solve problems as part of the process.

At the core of PBL is the principle that students are active learners who gain skills to become critical-thinkers. They are self-directed in their learning endeavors, stimulated, challenged, and prepared for their future.

"To teach is to touch the future."

LESSON PLAN

Goal - To become familiar with the tenets of problem-based learning(PBL) as a teaching/learning methodology.

Objectives:
To define PBL as a teaching/learning philosophy and method.
To review the history of PBL in education.
To report advantages of using PBL.
To develop strategies to overcome potential problems in PBL.

Pre-Opening:
"Do you think success in school is the result of ability or effort?"
Ask participants to reflect on this question, think about the answer, and turn to the next person for a four minute discussion. Share responses with group.

I. Introduction
Tell group what they have just done is experience PBL. They participated so were active, not passive, there is no one right answer to the question posed, and the teacher is not the authority. Their answer and the justification were OK.

Americans differ from Asians in their overall response to this question. Americans favor ability, and Asians believe effort is a major contributor to success.

II. Body
What is PBL?
Why use PBL?
How can potential problems be overcome?

III. Conclusion

Review

Resources:

WORKSHEET

What could PBL offer you as a teacher?

What benefits are there for the learners?

What process can you use to transform one of your current sessions into a PBL format?

What barriers do you anticipate?

How can they be overcome?

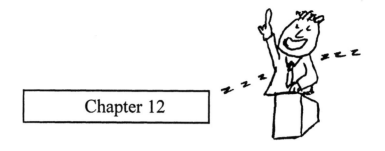

Chapter 12

EFFECTIVE PRESENTATIONS

I once saw a funny cartoon depicting cowboys and horses tossed together in a tangled mess in the middle of a street in an old western town. The caption read, "How many times do I have to tell you, a posse is something you have to organize?"

The main focus of this chapter is to describe a process that allows you to deliver an effective presentation because you have taken time to plan and organize. This may occur in a formal setting either giving a presentation or teaching a group of students. The process starts with thinking about what you will do, then moves into the preparation that takes place before you deliver your presentation, and concludes with an evaluation of what you did.

There are four steps to follow when delivering a presentation:

1. Planning
2. Preparation
3. Delivery
4. Evaluation

Careful attention to each of these steps will assuage your anxiety and reduce most fears of giving a presentation.

PLANNING

The planning step establishes the framework for your class, session, or presentation. What is the topic? Determine the overall purpose of the session. Decide what the objectives are for the session. Base this on what it is the students will know, skills they will be able to accomplish, or attitudes they will form as a result of the session. The actual process of writing objectives is described in Chapter 7. The objectives are the intended outcomes that will result from your presentation.

Think about what the "take home" message is. This is based on identifying what major concept you want to get across. Determine what principles or theories this concept is based on.

Decide what it is you want to teach. Think in broad concepts. In this step, you will need to also decide what NOT to teach. Is there enough time to accomplish what you want to? Depending on the depth of each point, 3-9 points can be covered in a straight hour of lecture. The more breaks for interaction in a presentation, the fewer points can be made.

For example:

        lecture = 9 points
        group discussion = 4 points
        demonstration and practice session = 1 point

Now develop a tentative outline which will help you organize your thoughts and content. An outline provides a written structure to your topic. The outline also helps you determine the sequence of the information. Types of outlines include:

1. Classical
        subsections
        main points
        examples
2. Problem-centered
        step-by-step
        possible solutions
3. Sequential
        historical events
        logical order - one point leads to the next
        familiar to the unfamiliar

"Yes, Jane Lyons of Seaside, Massachusetts, sitting next to Dale Harmon, Class of '96, it is important for a writer to know his audience."

Figure 9 - Know your audience.

Analyze your audience:

What is their background?
How many are there?
What is the room or environment like that they will be in?
What expectations does the audience have?
What is the level of knowledge?
What is the age range?
What language barriers exist?
What related experience have they had?
Are they voluntarily attending, or is it mandated?
How heterogeneous is the group?

Items to consider relative to content:

Is depth of content based on what is already known?
Is the content relevant to them?
How can you make it interesting?
How can you involve the students in the learning process?
What current events can be incorporated? What examples, metaphors, or analogies can be used to help make it relevant?
Did you research the topic thoroughly so you are familiar and comfortable with it?

The classroom is a dynamic, everchanging and often unpredictable interaction. For those reasons, do not over plan; build in flexibility. Blessed are those who are flexible, for they shall not be bent out of shape.

In summary, the planning step includes key elements of synthesizing the materials you have collected, organizing the material into a sequence, and developing an outline to fit the audience and the purpose of the session.

PREPARATION

The efforts resulting from the preparation step are evident when you deliver. Mark Twain, noted author and lawyer said, "It takes three weeks to prepare a good ad lib argument."

After careful planning, you are ready to select how to teach and determine which methods you will use.

The methods you use will be based on:

your skill at using various methods
the objectives of the session
the time available-is it a block or continuous or one time only?
the number of people
the room arrangement or environment (chairs, equipment)
your teaching style and the students' learning styles

No one method of teaching has been identified as the best way to teach. Look for ways to provide a variety of methods as suggested in Chapter 7. A change of pace is necessary every 15-20 minutes, about the length of a good sermon. In addition to changing methods, you can change the pace by moving around the room. Asking questions, writing, using visuals, and giving assignments that provide students a chance to interact in small buzz groups all provide breaks. Consider how you will interact and involve the students. Interaction is like voting in Chicago: "Do it early and do it often."

Next, acquire your needed resources and materials; the items intended to supplement the verbal presentation. Options include videotapes, slides, overhead transparencies, films, and computer-aided instructional devices. Determine what audio visuals (AV) will add. They are not simply "window dressing" but should serve a definite purpose. Refer to Chapter 14 for more information on effective design and use of AV.

Decide what kind of notes you will use. I recommend using notes. I use the analogy that I never fly without a net much like a trapeze artist. Notes provide you security and organization and how you use them is important.

Use an outline format to allow for spontaneity and a conversational tone of voice. High light the points in your notes that you want to emphasize. Leave white space to make notes to yourself and use different fonts to help draw your attention to key points.

It is OK to read your notes. It is OK to refer to them to locate your place, or to review them to be sure you have included everything you intended. Reading notes briefly is acceptable. The danger is in prolonging the reading because you will lose eye contact with the students. Also, prolonged reading encourages a more monotone voice, and you want to avoid that because it lulls the students to inattention. Nearly everyone recognizes that his or her natural speaking voice is different than the reading voice. Try speaking naturally into a tape recorder and then try reading a prepared script. Listen to the two tapes and note any differences, especially in voice tone and inflection.

Practice your presentation to allow you to become familiar with the material as well as the order of it. Use the run through to get a sense of the timing as well. Coordinate what you say with visuals, props, and other supporting materials. The rehearsal gives you an opportunity to make any modifications and it allows you to act confidently when you give the actual presentation. Find someone who can act as a critic and give you honest feedback.

The preparation step cannot be underestimated. Abraham Lincoln is remembered as a great speaker. The Gettysburg Address was only 10 sentences--271 words. These words, however, went through five drafts and resulted only after two weeks of thought and preparation.

DELIVERY

The basics of giving a presentation are offered here. Recommendations for making your sessions come alive are found in Chapter 13 on Dynamic Delivery.

Confidently approach the area where you position yourself. Get your notes and materials settled, take a deep breath to relax, look up and smile at the group. Proceed to a pre-opening. This engages the audience and establishes rapport. How do you get their attention? Some teachers start by saying "It's time to get started." Some say "This meeting is called to order." Some whistle. Some stand mute at the podium hoping the students will notice and stop talking on their own accord. The pre-opening is designed to gain the student's attention and interest immediately.

Some techniques are:

> ask a question that the session will answer
> start by posing a dilemma
> give an alarming statistic
> tell an intriguing story or anecdote
> relate the content to students' experiences or future career
> place the material in a historical setting
> indicate how the material fits with previous or future sessions
> use a dramatic picture or drawing or cartoon

I sometimes show a slide of a serene picture (a snow capped mountain or a quiet lake for example) accompanied by classical music. This is soothing and helps relax students by letting them sweep aside distractions and anxieties and mentally prepare for the session ahead. When the music stops, it is a signal that it is time to get started.

Vary your beginning. Make it fit with the content by being related and appropriate, and make it fit with your STYLE.

There are three major sections in a presentation:
1. opening
2. body
3. closing

Opening

Use the blackboard as a table of contents or a tour guide. This provides a focus for the students as well as a visual structure of the class. This strategy also helps students with note taking. Writing key concepts on the board helps with the pace of the class. The first five minutes set the stage, so use this time to project your energy and enthusiasm to grab the group's attention right away.

There are three points to cover in your opening which provides an overview:

1. Today's session will cover a, b, and c (key points)
2. This is important because .... (relevancy)
3. At the end of the session you will......know, do, feel (objectives)

There are two great opportunities for making an impact on your audience, and the opening is one time. It serves to motivate the group and to seque into the main points.

Body

Build the content around the objectives you present. Relate key points to the central focus and purpose. Be sure you make transitions between various parts. Tie things together; do not leave items fragmented for the students. Provide examples and frequently use the words, "It's like...."

Closing

This is the second time for you to make a strong impact on the audience. Restate the focus or purpose, and summarize the key concepts. You can refer back to the board where you wrote these during your opening and now reinforce them. Or erase the board and have the students give a summary. This technique provides feedback to you to help gauge if students got the main points and can demonstrate an understanding of those points.

If you say, "And finally" or "In conclusion" the group begins to leave, either by physically getting up, or mentally by tuning out what you are saying. Because the closing is an important time to reinforce key information, your goal is to keep their attention until you are ready to close. A good way to do that is to put up a list on the board for students to copy or state a list of ideas. This will keep them from packing up and preparing to exit the room prematurely.

Clarify, usually through questions the students pose, any concepts or items that remain unclear. You can easily incorporate the 3 x 5 inch cards whereby students who are reluctant to orally ask questions out of fear of appearing uninformed or stupid, can more freely ask questions by writing them down.

Inform the group what it is they need to do between this session and the next one. This serves as a reminder and also brings official closure to the session.

Avoid closings that are jejune. Plan the closing wisely. Saying, "that's all for today" or "we're out of time" not only lack imagination, but are unacceptable because you forfeit an opportunity to make an impact.

EVALUATION

Evaluation can function in two ways: 1) measuring how you did as a teacher and 2) measuring the students' understanding of the information presented. Looking at yourself is necessary to improve or to enhance what you have done. Chapter 15 provides more information on evaluation. The process is to formulate the questions to be asked, collect the data and analyze it, and make any modifications indicated.

As soon as possible after each session ask yourself and make note of your answers to these questions:

What did students respond to?
What went well?
What did I do best?
What were the problems?
Note items for:
Next time I want to ...
I want to try ...

Self-reflection and evaluation described above is essential. However, you are also continually evaluating during a session by noting students' reactions. Not all evaluation is done with paper and pencil if you remain alert to the students.

Video your presentation and view it privately, or ask for input from your colleagues as another form of evaluation.

Invite a colleague into your session and confer with him or her after the session to get feedback. This is good for content as well as teaching techniques.

Keep a journal where you record notes about the session. Include notes on items such as was there enough time, or how effective were the visuals, or what did the students learn?

Audio record a session to capture your voice. You can also do this before a session to critique yourself or make comparisons.

Another way of evaluating is to involve the students. Ways to do this include:

a committee of students
cards left at the door
quality circles
written questionnaires

The final step is to take what you have learned through the experience and the feedback obtained, and incorporate those ideas into the next session! Simply collecting the information is only half the job.

In summary, effective presentations are developed in advance through a process of planning that focuses on establishing the content for the session. This involves synthesizing the materials you have collected, organizing the materials into a sequence, and developing an outline. The next step of preparation includes determining which methods to use to deliver the information. Several factors influence this decision including: the characteristics of the audience, your abilities, the objectives of the session, and the resources you have available. Next, consider the actual delivery of the content in an orderly manner. Explore the possibilities for a pre-opening that will capture the group's attention and make them interested in what will follow. The opening of any session is when you reveal the agenda for the presentation. You are not giving away any secrets or surprise elements here, only setting the stage for the session and preparing the audience's frame of mind. The body follows logically, and you conclude with a review and a summary that brings closure to the session. Finally, evaluating what you have done is essential. You need to know where you have been and how effective you were to determine where to go next. Use a variety of ways suggested for collecting and analyzing the information. You have proceeded initially mentally, then carefully on paper, and now you are ready to add the punch to create the live action.

> "I have come to the conclusion that failing in the classroom as a professor may be the best way to improve the quality of teaching and learning...It is the process of risk-taking, experimentation, failure, reflection and continued exploration that is the hallmark of creativity, inventiveness, and even successful teaching." (Chiodo, 1989)

LESSON PLAN

Goal - To make your delivery more vibrant by maximizing the preparation process.

Objectives:
To comprehend the four steps in designing a presentation.
To manage the preparation process in a systematic, organized manner.
To increase confidence through organization.

Pre-Opening:
By the end of today's session, you will be able to name the 5 Bs of Speaking.
  Be prepared
  Be sincere
  Be humorous
  Be brief
  Be seated

I. Introduction
Activity: Recall a time when you were teaching and either before, during, or after, you entertained the idea that "it" did not go well.

Now recall a good experience you had teaching.

Determine those elements that made it good.

What elements suggested it needed improvement or elimination?

How can you correct or eliminate the ideas that were less than expected?

Things revealed in this process should lead to the very things that will be remedied by using the four steps in the process described.

III. Conclusion:
Everyone has experienced the flutter of butterflies in their stomachs when they speak. However, by using the steps described today in this session, YOU CAN TRAIN THOSE BUTTERFLIES TO *FLY* IN ORDER!

WORKSHEET

What steps are used to develop a session or presentation?

What are the three parts of each presentation and what is included in each part?

What tips and techniques can you use to make a presentation effective?

How can you evaluate and improve a session?

Chapter 13

DYNAMIC DELIVERY

"A message ineffectively delivered is a message ignored!"

Tauber (1992)

ADDING POWER TO A PRESENTATION

You probably have heard that speaking to a group is feared by more people than death! Actually, fear of snakes ranks higher than both. If you experience a dry mouth, trembling, cold limbs, or a sense of anxiety, there are reasons. The hormone adrenaline signals your brain to go on alert as a protection mechanism from danger. This is an extreme reaction however, and a certain amount of tension or nervousness can help you do your best in front of any group. This is because nervousness produces energy, and if it is directed, it can be beneficial. Controlling nerves and the fear generated can be done without therapy or medications.

I can help you with the skills for delivering a presentation, but it is your responsibility to add your personality. Your personality makes the material come ALIVE and makes your style unique. This chapter provides information in seven categories. Gaining skills in these areas will put power in any presentation.

There are three essential elements in your delivery to make it dynamic.

CONVICTION - A great teacher has intensity and communicates it -- not with a contrived act, but a genuine, authentic presentation of the person. You want to be genuine, be connected, and be involved with the group.

Subject mastery is a basic requirement, but is knowing the subject content enough to teach it? No. Knowledge by itself is insufficient. Knowing the subject content is a basic requirement, but it is also the bare minimum. Teachers must also have the skill to formulate goals and objectives, to use effective teaching methods, to encourage active involvement by students, and to construct valid evaluation measures. Dynamic teachers establish high expectations, they inspire and stimulate students, and they get actively involved with their students.

ENERGY - Personality does play a role in style. Your personality communicates who you are. Just be yourself. Well, not exactly; it is helpful to develop a teaching self. You must hold the attention of a group by using a variety of devices, similar to an actor on stage.

Self-disclosure can be used to project your personality. When you carefully call attention to yourself to demonstrate points, you allow students to see that you are human. Using yourself as the focal point of a joke is also better than picking on a student, who may not see the humor, or be offended.

ENTHUSIASM - "In the classroom, an instructor's enthusiasm is often contagious; so too, is the lack of enthusiasm." (McKeachie, 1974). Students deem enthusiasm to be the most important trait the teacher brings to the classroom. Develop enthusiasm as a strong component of your teaching style. Strive for a somewhat dramatic style. Most students seem to appreciate drama and it holds their attention. It also becomes memorable. If you are excited about the presentation and the content, it helps students become excited and interested.

When attempting to develop enthusiasm, it may be somewhat difficult to actually describe what it is because of its abstract nature. To help you get your arms around enthusiasm, check out the descriptions at the end of this chapter.

SEVEN POWERFUL ADDITIONS

Paying attention to the following areas will provide the power and the punch necessary to captivate your group. An imaginative presentation will be the result of your effort.

Body Language

Communicating in the classroom or during a presentation is done with more than words. People can speak about 125 words/minute, but people think or listen much faster, about 400 words/minutes. This allows people spare time to take a break from listening and gives them an opportunity to look at what else is going on. So, they look at you when they are not occupied with listening, more than 50% of the time. In fact, words account for only 7% of the message. The vocal tone accounts for 38%, but 55% of the message is conveyed visually through the non-verbal communication process. Your body language is used to stimulate visually and to relate to others nonverbally.

Body language, the relationship between body movements and communication, is called kinesics. Body language for some is instinctive, but it can be learned and it can be imitated. You want to acknowledge body language so you can monitor and control it, to interpret its meaning, and to change if necessary to help you function effectively in your delivery. Body language is a powerful component of what you communicate.

Animation involving hand gestures is encouraged so you are not perceived as boring or stiff. Gestures transmit to the students your enthusiasm, make the material more interesting, and can be entertaining. They need to be meaningful and natural, not nervous and tentative. Match your gestures to the size of the audience; large groups respond to big, sweeping gestures. Petite gestures may be missed entirely in an auditorium of 300 people. Small intimate gestures correspond to small groups.

How you stand creates a visual image of your personality. Some examples are:

hands in pockets
folded across chest (stern parent)
white-knuckle podium clutch
arms folded over lower front (fig leaf)
hands in the back (military parade rest)

Less severe positions are more inviting. When standing, lean slightly forward to communicate to students that you are approachable, receptive, and friendly. Placing one foot slightly ahead of the other also keeps some speakers from rocking or swaying side to side. Use appropriate gestures and resist the urge to simply periodically wave your arms around. A nod of the head conveys to students that you are listening and can also indicate positive reinforcement for ideas.

Eye contact is the most commonly used form of body language. Develop good eye contact as a matter of habit. Good eye contact connects you with the group, and shrinks the physical distance between you. Techniques for using good eye contact include focusing on someone different every 10-20 seconds. Or, after you finish your thought, move your eye contact to another person. If you shift too rapidly, it suggests a nervousness and comes across as darting eyes. It is easy to focus on the people directly in front of you or in the center of the room. Make a conscious effort to turn your head and look to the right and left, and front and back of the room. If you look at the ceiling like you were taught in speech class, remember everyone else was also taught that, so they all know it does not work!

The face of the teacher as well as the student is part of nonverbal communication. Facial expressions convey emotions. You receive valuable feedback by watching the facial expressions of your students. My experience has been that when I find a friendly face in a group, it increases my confidence and inspires me to better performance. Touching any part of your face is distracting. Be consciously aware of this and avoid this mannerism.

A key concept to remember about body language is that too much emphasis in any one area is distracting. Strive for a balance, rather than overkill. Retain the professional integrity of teaching.

How you look and what you wear is part of your body language message. Your appearance is more than the clothes you wear. Remember, the most important thing you can wear is a SMILE. Smiling is contagious and students generally react favorably and are more attentive, which helps them learn more.

Voice

Your voice conveys the emotional connotations of your message. The use of language is important and teachers must bring together the language of a discipline with the language of the students. Also important is the pace you use. At times you will slow down the tempo to project clarity. At times your pace will speed up for emphasis. Be aware that most people can listen one and a half times the normal speaking rate of 125 words per minutes. To bridge this gap, contrast in the speed is helpful.

The volume you use also varies. Mark your notes to remind yourself to lower or raise your voice. This will help you avoid sounding monotone. For large groups, or for soft spoken teachers, use a microphone to project your voice. A lavaliere mike on your lapel allows you to move around. Test the mike in advance by gently tapping on it. Blowing into a microphone can cause damage from the moisture inherent in your breathe. Other voice elements to pay attention to are tone, pitch, rhythm and inflection. The voice is more than sounds organized into words. Your level of confidence is projected when speaking. Your degree of involvement in what you say while speaking is also projected.

Silence and the Pause

Using a pause can be effective if you know when to use a pause. Remember this: "All speakers pause to breath, good speakers pause to punctuate." Pause for a deep breath to help you relax. Pauses allow the audience to take a brief break for reflection.

Speakers can lose their place or forget what comes next. Recall the Chinese proverb: The palest ink is better than the best memory. Use your notes to locate your place.

If you cannot think what to say next, say nothing. Silence is more effective than using uhs, errs, uhms. You may not realize you are using these nonwords. It is helpful to audio record a presentation or session so you become aware of how frequent and annoying these nonwords become.

Space

Space is another area you can focus on to bring the element of drama to your presentation. The configuration of the classroom helps determine 'the psychological climate. In the movie *Dead Poets Society* (1989) teacher Robin Williams climbed on top of his desk to drive home the message that students need to look at life from a different perceptive. I use that film clip very effectively to prompt teachers to be creative with space. Another scene shows Mr. Williams reading passages from a book. He does not read hidden behind a lectern, but rather by sitting at eye level with the students.

Aristotle, the great teacher, was given to walking as he taught. His peripatetic style reminds us it is possible to discourse while moving from place to place, being careful not to nervously pace, however. Students observe how you sit, stand, and walk. Moving around is key to retain the students' interest because it attracts attention and their eyes follow your movement. Also, by making use of all the classroom space available, you will generally be more animated.

Environment

How desks or chairs are arranged is an important aspect of environment. You want to seek maximum student-teacher interaction and use arrangements that foster eye contact. If you insist on having students sit in rows where your access to them is limited and they spend most of their time staring at the back of someone's head, you may be better suited to working with sardines. In the factory, it is important that the sardines be lined up in neat, straight rows in the can, but not in a classroom.

Props

In the movie *Stand and Deliver* (1988), Jamie Escalante, the Los Angeles teacher used an apple, a chef's apron and a knife to demonstrate the concept of fractions to the math students. I use this film clip to indicate how materials and props add a visual dimension to teaching.

You can also dress for a role and adopt the persona of another person. Simple props can help set the mood for the session. I once role played Ben Franklin wearing his artisan leather apron and half glasses, and I received raves from my classmates. It was one of my memorable moments in graduate school.

ENTHUSIASM RATING CHART*

Categories	LOW			MEDIUM		HIGH	
	(1)	(2)	(3)	(4)	(5)	(6)	(7)
1. Vocal Delivery	Monotone, minimum inflections, little variation in speech, poor articulation.			Pleasant variations of pitch, volume and speed; good articulation.		Great and sudden changes from rapid, excited speech to a whisper; varied tone and pitch.	
2. Eyes	Looked dull or bored; seldom opened eyes wide or raised eyebrows; avoids eye contact; often maintains a blank stare.			Appeared interested; occasionally lighting up, shining, opening wide.		Characterized as dancing, snapping, shining, lighting up frequently, opening wide, eyebrows raised; maintains eye contact while avoiding staring.	
3. Gestures	Seldom moved arms out toward person or object; never used sweeping movements; kept arms at side or folded, rigid.			Often pointed, occasional sweeping motion using body, head, arms, hands, and face; maintained steady pace of gesturing.		Quick and demonstrative movements of body, head, arms, hands and face.	

---

* Enthusiasm Rating chart was developed by Mary L. Collins, 1976.

Category			
4. Body Movement	Seldom moved from one spot, or from sitting to standing position; sometimes "paces" nervously.	Moved freely, slowly, and steadily.	Large body movements, swung around, walked rapidly, changed pace; unpredictable and energetic; natural body movements.
5. Facial Expression	Appeared deadpan, expressionless or frowned; little smiling, lips closed.	Agreeable; smiled frequently; looked pleased, happy, or sad if situation called for.	Appeared vibrant, demonstrative; showed many expressions; broad smile; quick, sudden changes in expression.
6. Word Selection	Mostly nouns, few descriptors or adjectives; simple or trite expressions.	Some descriptors or adjectives or repetition of the same ones.	Highly descriptive, many adjectives, great variety.
7. Acceptance of Ideas and Feelings	Little indication of acceptance or encouragement; may ignore students' feelings or ideas.	Accepted ideas and feelings; praised or clarified; some variations in response, but frequently repeated same ones.	Quick to accept, praise, encourage, or clarify; many variations in response; vigorous nodding of head when agreeing.
8. Overall Energy Level	Lethargic; appears inactive, dull or sluggish.	Appeared energetic and demonstrative sometimes, but mostly maintained an even level.	Exuberant; high degree of energy and vitality; highly demonstrative.

(Adapted from *Practical Applications of Research*, PHI DELTA KAPPA Newsletter, June 1981).

A word of caution: Don't rely too heavily on the results of only one observation. Repeated observations will enable you and your observer to evaluate the level of enthusiasm. Try changing your low-enthusiasm performance to high by practicing to improve your lower-rated categories of behavior. In general, a score of 8-20 = dull or unenthusiastic level; 21-42 = moderate level of enthusiasm; 43-56 = very high level of enthusiasm.

Humor

Humor is sometimes overlooked as an effective tool in teaching. However, you should use humor. Laughter is like internal jogging. Humor in a presentation projects your attitude. It also signals a friendly environment which facilitates learning.

Additionally, humor has other purposes in the classroom. It provides:

1. a tension and stress release
2. creativity to loosen fixed positions and open the mind
3. bonding to lessen hostility
4. enjoyment of learning
5. relief from boredom

When asked about humor, 50% of instructors said they use humor, usually by telling three or four jokes. Another 40% used funny stories over jokes. Anecdotes or illustrations that make a point are sources of humor. Tell jokes on yourself rather than potentially offending others. Wit, puns, and satire are relatively easy to include in a presentation. Avoid using sarcasm as humor. Students generally fail to find it funny.

With any type of humor, keep in mind:

1. propriety - sensitivity
2. timing - must be related to the content
3. aspiration - do you have the confidence? Make humor part of your repertoire.

The University of Florida, Institute of Food and Agricultural Sciences (Warnock, 1987) developed ten levels of humor, based on the degree of risk involved.

1. Appreciates but can't use easily
2. Laughs readily with self and others
3. Shares cartoons and funny stories
4. Recounts humor from past life
5. Plays practical jokes
6. Tells jokes
7. Uses magic, puppetry, clowning and storytelling

8. Uses humor spontaneously
9. Acts as master of ceremonies
10. Works as a comedian

Cartwright (1993) suggests teachers:
Approach humor as a learnable skill. Read about it, listen to it, watch it, practice it, try it, and stumble through it. Through this process you will become funnier.

Be sensitive to the feelings of your students. Humor at the expense of others has no place in the classroom. Fit the humor in with your style and the subject. Unrelated jokes distract from the subject matter. Use humor to supplement other teaching strategies, to grab and focus students. Start a humor file. Introducing cartoons that relate to what is being learned and carry a message, is fun and easy and relatively low risk humor. When you use cartoons, enlarge them for better visibility and use them with the proper acknowledgement. Most are copyright protected.

Attempting to introduce all the elements presented in this section can be overwhelming. You may feel yourself whirling like laundry in a clothes dryer. Choose a couple of the elements that can add power to any presentation, and work at developing those. Once mastered, you will feel comfortable introducing them into your presentations. Then continue adding the others. When you make a conscious effort and practice, these additions feel natural and become a habit. Soon you will find that the power you add to make your presentations dynamic has also empowered your group to learn better.

"Nothing great was ever accomplished without enthusiasm."

-Emerson

LESSON PLAN

Goal - To add power to any presentation by incorporating good delivery principles.

Objectives:
To identify seven categories that enliven presentations.
To gain skills and techniques in each area.

Pre-Opening:
Show transparency of sleeping students. Ask for reactions from group members. Why do they think this situation happens? What could be done to avoid this classroom scene?

I. Introduction

You have spent a lot of time and effort in planning and preparing a presentation. What are some of the things you have done in the process? It is not enough to organize the information; you also need skills to deliver the message. Identifying those skills and developing techniques in seven areas is the focus of this session. Being aware of the seven areas will allow you to develop skills in each area and enable you to deliver a powerful presentation. Using the techniques discussed will not only keep people awake, but alert, interested, and able to learn.

II. Body

A. What adds POWER?
Develop the ideas resulting from initial question. Each member of the group can contribute to the discussion of each item based on what has worked effectively for them.
Add items from this chapter if they are not produced by group.
B. Demonstrate skills
Ask group members to demonstrate their ideas using the various skills.

III. Conclusion

Resources: Flip chart or board to record POWER ideas.

WORKSHEET

Is knowledge of the subject enough to be an effective presenter?

Why develop delivery skills?

What seven areas can add power to a presentation?

Name key points or techniques to include from each area.

Videotape one of your presentations. In which of the areas do you have good skills?

Which areas do you want to improve your skills and how can you do it?

Chapter 14

AUDIO VISUALS

Remember 30% Hear
Remember 30 % See
Remember 45% See & Hear

The example above shows that combining verbal and visual communications can increase the learners' retention of information by 50% compared
to using either alone.

No one media or visual is right for every situation or every purpose.
This chapter exposes you to various types of visuals, presents techniques
for designing and using common visuals, and provides overall criteria for
judging the value of the media used.

I like to play golf. In my golf bag I have several golf clubs because I
cannot use the same club for every shot. Each club is designed for a specific
situation and distance. The club I use depends on the variables of the
situation. It is the same idea when you select which audio visual (AV) to
use. Because no one visual is right in all cases, you have a variety to select
from based on the variables of the situation.

WHY USE AV?

Visuals are not just "window dressing," but serve a purpose. They:

1. help tell a story
2. appeal especially to visual learners - 70% of learners are visual
3. add interest and capture and hold attention
4. reinforce the verbal message
5. present images, pictures, graphics that are not possible by hearing alone
6. add variety to a presentation
7. stimulate discussion
8. broaden the experience for the learner beyond "hearing"
9. are used to gain focus
10. emphasize, clarify, or summarize key points
11. organize presentation so both learner and teacher can follow

So why are visuals not used more often? Presenters and teachers may have concern that:

Farcus   by David Waisgla
                          Gordon Coulth

MULTIMEDIA TRADE SHOW

WAISGLASS/COULTHART   © 1995 Farcus Cartoons/dist. by Universal Press Syn

"Due to technical difficulties, Sammy th puppet will tell you all about computer assisted learning."

1. AV materials take time to prepare

2. they may lack expertise and/or equipment required

3. cost may not be justified

4. if organized ahead of time, AV can limit spontaneity of the experience

TYPES OF AV

The question is not should I use audio visuals, but what audio visuals should I use? Common choices are:

Slides	Flip chart
Chalkboard	Handouts
Overhead transparencies	Models
Videos	Computers
*Films	*Audiotapes

*Like other visuals, these provide a change pictorially, but also add the dimension of hearing by interjecting another voice into the room.

Some questions regarding how you decide are:

What is the cost
How much time and expertise are needed to prepare
What impact do you want the AV to make
What is the ease of retrievability and use
What is the shelf life, and what storage issues are there
What level of interactivity is created?

Overhead transparencies rank high in most areas except on impact.
To use AV effectively, you need skill both in designing and in delivering AV. Assistance on designing slides and transparencies is included on the following pages. Criteria for evaluating your visuals is also presented.

DELIVERY SKILLS

Overall delivery skills are:

1. Know how to use the equipment. Test the sound and focus ahead of time.
2. Always have a spare light bulb.
3. Preview all videos and films before using. Note time.
4. Set the stage for students by discussing points to watch for, relate video or films to objectives, and alert students to new vocabulary.
5. When using a film or video, weigh the merits of the visual for its ability to teach some worthwhile lesson, point, or objective. After showing, evaluate the film through proper discussion to determine what was learned.
6. To load slides in a tray, use the "thumb spot" technique. Assemble slides in correct order. Number each in sequence. Then place a dot at the lower left corner of the slide mount. Load the slides in numerical sequence in the tray, turning each one upside down so the dot is under your right thumb in the upper right corner and facing you. When the tray is correctly loaded, all dots are visible at the top

outer edge of the tray. Another technique is to load slides into the tray in order. Take a colored marker and run it along the top edge. If the slides are out of order, the resulting crooked line will indicate it.

7. When showing slides, "Drain, then explain." Review the entire slide, then go back over each point and provide the explanation.

8. Allow 1-3 minutes per visual. Turn off equipment when not using it to redirect attention back to speaker.

9. Use a pencil to write information on a flip chart in advance. During the presentation, use a felt marker (never yellow because it is too light to project) to write over it boldly. Not only will you look brilliant as you appear to recall the information off the top of your head, but this technique allows you to be neat, organized, and remember all important points. Doing this ahead of time frees your mind from this task and allows you to focus more on the group.

10. A transparency projects just as you see it. Read or take cues from the transparency rather than looking back at the screen. One advantage of using an overhead projector is that you face the audience and maintain eye contact.

11. Progressive disclosure is a technique of using a sheet of paper to cover some content, and disclosing only a portion at a time. This technique allows you and the audience to focus on one point at a time. Place paper under rather than over the transparency to prevent it from blowing or falling onto the floor.

12. When using an overhead projector, practice using a pointer, not your finger. Point to the transparency, not the screen.

13. Add information with a marker pen during class to allow for input and interaction. Ideas developed spontaneously in class create an informal, participative setting.

14. Keep lights on for overheads and videos. Slides and films generally require darker rooms, which improves visibility, but reduces eye contact.

Regardless of the type of AV you create, follow these two design principles:

1. Make it legible
2. Make it organized

The level of sophistication or elaborate design you choose is influenced by several factors as indicated:

C-Level Production	B-Level Production	A-Level Production
	AUDIENCE MOOD	
Receptive		Hostile
	AUDIENCE SIZE	
Small		Large
	BUDGET	
Limited		Flexible
	CONTENT	
Pick-up		Original
	DELIVERY SYSTEM	
Common		Unique
	DESIRED RESULT	
Awareness		Action
	EXPECTATIONS	
Flexible		State-of-the-art
	ROLE	
Supportive		Stand-alone
	SCHEDULE	
Imposed		Open-ended
	SHELF LIFE	
Short		Long
	SUBJECT MATTER	
Simple		Complex
	USAGE	
One-time		Multiple

Sandy (1990)

MAKING AND USING VISUAL MATERIALS

1. *KEEP THEM SIMPLE*

   The first precept in visuals is simplicity-in lettering, art, amount of wording, and ideas. Keep to the essentials. Avoid clutter; visualize one element of a subject at a time. Avoid distractions; too many gimmicks spoil the presentation.

2. *BE CREATIVE - USE IMAGINATION*

   Any idea can be visualized if you use your creative imagination. Adapt common objects to tell your story. Improvise. Think positively.

3. *MAKE THE MOST OF WHAT YOU HAVE*

   Think in terms of things easy to get, or things already on hand. Demonstrate materials a specialist uses in the field, pictures from magazines, art work from a poster, letters made from colored marking tape, 5 and 10 or hardware store items. Raid the children's toy box. I recall two simple, yet effective visuals: 1) an orthopedic surgeon used a picture of the spine for an entire presentation, 2) a church school teacher placed a clear pie plate filled with blue food colored water on an overhead projector, and created "waves" by gently moving the pie plate, and added models of fish.

4. *MAKE VISUALS SERVE A PURPOSE*

   Don't use visuals for the sake of having visuals. Before using a visual, ask yourself how it helps tell the story. If it doesn't, cut it. If you do not explain a visual you use, or if it fails to explain a point, don't use it.

5. USE VARIETY IN VISUALS

   Use different types of visuals to enhance and support your session. Don't get into a visual rut where students say, "Here comes the expert with the box of slides under his/her arm." You can vary pictures with real objects or models. Try for the unexpected to add drama to your presentation. Cast objects in new roles and ways.

6. *EXPLOIT SIZE, DEPTH, CONTRAST, DESIGN*

   Size is impressive. Use large, even wall-high charts which dwarf the speaker. Gain the effect of size and dimension by using depth devices in art, pictures, and charts. Use enough contrast in colors to aid visibility, but don't overdo it. Contrasts in size, as mentioned above, emphasize. Good artistic design is necessary in posters, photographs, and other visuals.

7. *USE VISUALS TO SIMPLIFY THE COMPLEX*
   Use visuals to simplify complex ideas and processes. Synchronizing sound and picture will often accomplish this.
8. *ILLUSTRATE IDEAS WITH "ALLEGORY VISUALS" FOR ADDED IMPACT*
   Use real objects or pictures to suggest unpicturable ideas: a picture of the Capitol in Washington to suggest congressional action, a close-up photo of a handful of soil to suggest "Mother Earth" or the heritage of the land, a rocket going up to symbolize progress, test tubes and microscopes to indicate research. Parable teaching is effective in the classroom, at a meeting, or on television.

Adapted from:
Instructional Resources Center
University of Minnesota
St. Paul, MN 55108

EFFECTIVE DESIGN OF SLIDES

1. Use horizontal rather than vertical slides
2. Limit slide to 7 lines of print - about 35 words
3. Use a readable print font - orator is good
4. Use CAPITAL LETTERS for emphasis, but not all CAPS - becomes hard to read
5. Double space between lines
6. Visibility is increased using white letters on blue or black letters on a yellow background
7. Keep it simple - about what you could read on a T-shirt
8. Use outline form - not complete sentences
9. Visualize the verbal - visual images enhance words

(Johnson & Burns, 1983)

TRANSPARENCY DESIGN TIPS

1. Limit each transparency to ONE key point
2. Limit content to 10 lines or less
3. Use 7 or fewer words per line
4. Limit columns or numbers to 3
5. Use letters 1/3 - 1/2" high for good legibility
6. Mount transparency with cardboard frame and write notes on edges
7. Professionalize with colors. Use overlay techniques which are impressive and also lower the cost because you need fewer transparencies.
8. Number the transparencies to keep them in order.
9. Transparencies made in advance are neater and organized and can be duplicated as handouts.
10. Transparencies can be reused thereby making them low cost to use and easy to store.

Adapted from:
Faculty Development Newsletter
December 1985, Vol. 1, No. 5
Dept. of Family Practice
(Medical College of Wisconsin, 1985).

WAYS OF LOOKING AT A BLACKBOARD

Blackboards may not even be black anymore, but they can still be effective as teaching aids for all teachers, not just math instructors.

The board can serve as a table of contents. Use it to write major topics and points that will be covered in the session. This will focus and alert the class. It provides a visual structure and allows students to follow along easier. It can serve as an outline to facilitate note taking.

The blackboard is an excellent sidekick. Use it to post key points of a discussion.

The board is an excellent explainer of difficult concepts. Viewing a scheme on the board is a good way to show relationships.

Use the board to summarize the key elements of the presentation. Or, erase the board, and ask students to summarize from memory or notes they have taken.

Blackboards help students cope with new vocabulary. Legibly writing the words helps students see the correct spelling as well.

(Garcia, 1991)

HANDOUT MATERIAL

There are two categories of handouts:
        material to be used during a presentation
        material intended to be read later
Keep in mind that you want to keep the focus on you, and not let the written materials distract the group.

Complicated subject matter often needs to be supplemented with charts and graphs to provide clarity.

An outline indicating key points can also help the group follow along and facilitates note taking. This can be a time saver. It also fosters the learners' ability to extrapolate and paraphrase key points in their own words.

Some handout material contains exercises or activities to be used during the session.

It is essential to have clearly printed materials and to have them arranged in order. Use different colored paper for different components. Number the pages.

Material designed to supply additional information, or sources for more information is distributed at the end of the presentation. You do not want participants or students to read rather than pay attention to what you have to say.

RULES OF THUMB FOR EVALUATING VISUALS

1. VISIBILITY
        Can your materials be seen?
2. STRUCTURE
        Have you used form, grouping, and continuity to good advantage?

3. ECONOMY
   Are your visuals too expensive?
4. TECHNIQUE
   Is method of presenting smooth?
5. APPEAL
   Do your visuals attract and hold attention?
6. CLARITY
   Can people understand your objectives?
7. FIDELITY
   Are your models faithful reproductions of the real things?
8. VALIDITY
   Are your statements sound and factual?
9. CREDIBILITY
   Will people believe the message your visuals tell?
10. TACTICS
    Have you used the most feasible approach to the subject in relation to this audience?

Instructional Resources Center
University of Minnesota
St. Paul, MN 55108

LESSON PLAN

Goal - To add power to your presentation with audio visual aids.

Objectives:
To become familiar with types of AV materials.
To state reasons to use AV in teaching.
To compare advantages of various media.
To develop skill in designing and using AV.

Pre-Opening:
Find the worst example you can of a transparency. Project it on the overhead and say, "This is an OH MY GOSH transparency!"
Ask the group to point out what is wrong with it.
Real life examples I have seen used far too often are to photocopy a   page from a book, or a chart with a gazillion numbers on it.
It can be effective to use negative examples to make a point.

I. Introduction
Today's session is designed to broaden your view of what constitutes AV. This information will help you avoid getting stuck in an AV rut. After identifying what AV exists, discussion will include how to effectively design various types of AV, and techniques for how to correctly use different kinds of AV.

II. Body
What was the world like before television? Because of the influence of television, the majority of people are visual learners. What other reasons are there for using audio visuals in a session or presentation?
Which AV do you use most often and why?
Provide examples of visuals. Have group respond or evaluate "good" and "needs improvement." Make recommendations based on design principles for those needing changes.
Have group design visuals for a session they will use soon.
Ask learners to demonstrate AV use principles for slides, using a pointer, progressive disclosure, etc.

III. Conclusion

Ask participants to name one type of AV they have not used before, but are willing to use now and state why?

Review principles of design.

Resources: Variety of AV projection equipment.
Examples of transparencies, slides, and flip charts for evaluation.

WORKSHEET

What types of AV are there?

What are the advantages of each type of AV?

Which type of AV do you use most often?

Why reasons exist for using AV?

List techniques for effectively using slides, transparencies, videos, and other forms of AV.

Identify skills you want to develop and practice using them.

Design transparencies or other AV for a session you are giving following the principles of good design.

Chapter 15

EVALUATING TEACHING

Evaluation done after the fact is like positioning the bull's eye target after you shoot your arrow!

This chapter will introduce the topic of evaluation and describe what it is and how it is useful to your teaching. The focus for evaluation is on the teaching and not on techniques for evaluating what the students learn, called impact or outcome evaluation.

EXPLORING HOW TO EVALUATE

If evaluation is thought of "to judge", that approach can be seen as negative and is one reason teachers fear the very word, often going to extreme measures to avoid any form of evaluation. When evaluation is viewed as pejorative, the emotional intensity created can be overwhelming and dissuade teachers from conducting evaluation. If you consider evaluation as a means "to examine" it has a friendly overtone. Evaluation is akin to assessment, a Latin word meaning "to sit down beside." What you want to do is assess your teaching so your actions assist learning.

Evaluation is a tool to help the teacher, just as objectives, lesson plans, and audio visuals are. Evaluation is a process of systematically collecting information to assess teaching and improve effectiveness. The purpose of evaluation is two-fold: to show you where you have been and to direct you to where you go next. It is like a roadmap. A second purpose is to help assess how and what you taught or, in fact to measure the results of the learning process. Two kinds of evaluation to consider: is the instructor the object of the evaluation or is the course design?

process. Two kinds of evaluation to consider: is the instructor the object of the evaluation or is the course design?

Evaluation is a continuous process that teachers conduct all the time, formally or informally, sometimes even unconsciously. It serves as a constant source of information that is useful in making decisions about education. What would happen if the weather bureau only read its instruments once a year? Likely, our weather information would not be very accurate. Evaluation, to be most useful, needs to be systematic. To get a "true picture" you want to avoid the camera approach where you "click here, click there" and only get a snapshot, rather than the whole picture.

Formative evaluation is conducted with the objective of obtaining data or feedback as you teach. This makes it possible to make any changes before the end of the session. It is a proactive process that provides data for decision-making. Summative evaluation is conducted at the end and is as the name suggests, a summary. These data cannot change what has already happened, but are used to provide direction for the future, or the next time you teach. Both serve a different purpose; both are necessary.

Example of course evaluations and teacher evaluation are provided at the end of this chapter.

Basic questions regarding evaluation need to be asked. A central question to evaluation is asking yourself, "What effect am I having on my students and their learning?" What is the purpose of the evaluation? What will be evaluated? Who will conduct the evaluation? What evaluation design will be used? When will evaluation take place?

Involve students in the evaluation. Seek their input as you teach and also as a summary at the end.

Mid-course or mid-session, ask the students to respond to:

What helps you learn?
Describe two or three strengths of this course.
Describe two or three strengths of the instructor.

What one change would you suggest for the course and for the instructor?

Then compile the data and inform students of the outcomes. Tell students you will also conduct a mid-course evaluation by commenting on what you like about the students and on what you would like to see improve.

Another way to evaluate and improve teaching is to conduct classroom research. The primary purpose is to get feedback from the students while their learning is in progress. It is a systematic study of collecting data about teaching, and then using that data to improve the student learning.

Ask a colleague to observe your teaching and give you feedback in the following areas:

Organization - this includes content as well as how the classroom is managed. Content clearly presented in structured format of introduction, body, and conclusion to meet objectives.

Knowledge - competent and up-to-date in content, displays confidence, provides relevant examples, and explains theory and difficult concepts.

Relationship with learners - encourages participation, gives feedback, listens, shows respect, and establishes rapport.

Methods and Audio Visuals - uses appropriate variety and displays good technique.

Body language, Voice, Eye Contact, Gestures, Humor, Enthusiasm, Conviction, Space, Props, and Energy.

In summary, the desired outcome of evaluation is to have a positive effect on learning. To be complete and to provide greater credibility, evaluation should include positive comments along with indications of any negative areas for improvement. Meritorious evaluation may enhance self-confidence, but offer nothing for you to work to develop or improve. Even-handed evaluations give a sense of what strengths can be built upon as well as what areas need more attention. Make ongoing evaluation a normal part of your teaching and appreciate the insights provided.

Consider the B- auto mechanic.

The student got an A in taking the engine apart, and a D for putting it back together. The two scores taken together gave that student a B-!!

Was it a balanced evaluation?

End of Course Evaluation

Develop a questionnaire that is clear and concise, probably no more than 20 questions. The focus is on the course and the content.
Here is a list I developed after reviewing dozens of forms. Use it with a scale of 1-6 with descriptors of strongly agree to strongly disagree.

COURSE EVALUATION

The course syllabus provided useful information regarding the course.

Course objectives were expressed clearly.

Stated objectives agreed with course content.

Course objectives were achieved.

Course responsibilities were clearly defined.

The requirements of the course were explained.

The teaching materials used in this course were helpful.

The course built understanding of concepts and principles.

Course material was valuable to my future career.

The course stimulated my thinking to achieve significant learning.

The course was intellectually challenging.

My knowledge of the subject increased as a result of this course.

Class activities and assignments assisted me in achieving the objectives.

The work required by this course assisted me in my learning.

Teaching methods were varied.

The course was interesting and held my attention.

The course appeared to be carefully planned.

The content was well organized.

INSTRUCTOR EVALUATION

My instructor displays a clear understanding of course topics.

My instructor consistently pursues course objectives.

My instructor uses well chosen teaching methods in this course.

My instructor displays enthusiasm while teaching.

My instructor seems well prepared for class.

My instructor makes good use of examples and illustrations.

My instructor fosters an understanding of concepts and principles.

Exams and assignments cover important points of the class.

My instructor is able to help me understand difficult materials.

My instructor evaluates often and provides help when needed.

My instructor fosters the concept of mutual respect in this class.

My instructor encourages a learning partnership.

My instructor has stimulated my thinking.

My instructor deals fairly and impartially with me.

My instructor helps me understand the practical application of content in this course.

SELF EVALUATION

What are some of the best things you do in your teaching?

Think of the best teachers you ever had. What did they do?

Describe an outstanding thing you did in the classroom and the effect it produced?

Describe something that did not go as expected.

What do you want to improve?

FACULTY PERFORMANCE RATING GUIDE

Instructions: Circle the answer that most clearly describes your performance in the last year.

Performance Factors	Excellent	Good	Fair	Poor	Awful
Communications	Talks with God	Talks with Angels	Talks to self	Argues with self	Loses Argument with self
Adaptability	Walks on water consistently	Walks on water in emergency	Washes with water	Drinks water	Passes water
Initiative	Stronger than a locomotive	Stronger than a bull elephant	Stronger than a bull	Shoots the bull	Smells like a bull
Timeliness	Faster than a speeding bullet	Fast as a speeding bullet	Not quite as fast as bullet	Would you believe a slow bullet?	Wounds self with bullet
Quality	Leaps tall buildings	Must take running start	Can leap short building	Crashes into building	Cannot see buildings

- adapted from J. Goodman (McGee and Goldstein, 1983)

LESSON PLAN

Goal - To embrace the process of evaluation as a part of teaching.

Objectives:
To state purpose of evaluation.
To differentiate two types of evaluation.
To compose content for evaluation forms.

Pre-Opening:
"When you aim for perfection you discover it's a moving target."

George Fisher

I. Introduction
"What do you think of when you hear the word 'evaluation'?"
The result of this discussion is to reframe evaluation as a friend, not a foe.
The benefits of engaging in evaluation will be explored and different methods of evaluation will be identified.

II. Body
Why evaluate?
Who can evaluate? self, students, supervisor, colleagues
When should you evaluate?
What are the two types: Formative - data collected during course, reviewed and needed changes can be made right away.
Summative: Data collected at end of course or presentation. Useful after reviewed to make decisions about future.
Have group share evaluation methods they use successfully.
Provide various evaluation forms and ask group to critique.

III. Conclusion

Resources: Various evaluation instruments.

WORKSHEET

Describe the process you use to evaluate your teaching?

What rewards have you receive from evaluation?

How often do you evaluate?

What do you do with the results?

Design the "ideal" teacher evaluation form.

What are some of the principles of evaluation to avoid in the process?

What new ideas will you include in your evaluation process?

Chapter 16

GENERAL CLIMATE SETTING

ESTABLISHING THE LEARNING ENVIRONMENT AND DEVELOPING COMMUNITY

"Ideas are like rabbits. You get a couple and learn how to handle them, and pretty soon you have a dozen."

- John Steinbeck

IDEA SECTION

This chapter is designed to provide teaching tips and climate setting examples. Included are ideas for helping students succeed.

REMEMBER STUDENT NAMES

Take Polaroid pictures of groups of five or six students the first day of class. Write their names of the bottom and review these until you become familiar with the names. When returning assignments, use the student's name. When asking questions, use their name. If you can not recall, especially in sessions with lots of students, just ask. Using their names helps build a relationship and encourages mutual respect.

Dealing with Answers to Essay Examinations

Prepare a set of model answers to the examination questions and provide each student with a copy when the exams are returned. This reduces the amount of time needed to explain how the question should have been answered. It also decreases the number of student complaints about the grading. Use actual student responses whenever possible. They appreciate the recognition.

Clarifying Grade Expectations

Students need to know that their grades reflect both effort and achievement. Teachers generally combine the subjective with the objective. Share with students the descriptions of "A" and "C" students, or develop your own version.

The "A" Student - An Outstanding Student

Attendance: "A" students have virtually perfect attendance. Their commitment to the class resembles that of the teacher.

Preparation: "A" students are prepared for each class. They always read the assignment in advance. Their attention to detail is such that they occasionally correct a slip made by the teacher.

Curiosity: "A" students show interest in what is happening in the class and in the subject. They look up or dig out additional information on anything they do not understand. They ask interesting questions and make thoughtful comments.

Retention: "A" students have retentive minds. They are able to connect past learning with the present. They bring a strong background to the class and are willing to share it.

Attitude: "A" students have a winning attitude. They have both the determination and the self-discipline to succeed. They show initiative. They are not asking you what they should do.

Talent: "A" students have something special. It may be exceptional intelligence and insight. It may be unusual creativity, organizational skills, commitment, or a combination. These gifts are evident to the teacher and usually to the other students as well.

Results: "A" students make high grades on tests. Their work is a pleasure to grade.

"C" Students - Average or Typical Student

Attendance: "C" students miss class frequently. They put other priorities ahead of academic work. In some cases, their health or constant fatigue renders them physically unable to keep up with the demands of high-level performance.

Preparation: "C" students prepare assignments consistently, but in a perfunctory manner. Their work may be sloppy or careless. At times, it is incomplete or late.

Attitude: "C" students are not visibly committed to the class. They participate reluctantly and without enthusiasm. Their body language often expresses boredom.

Talent: "C" students vary enormously in talent. Some have exceptional ability but show undeniable signs of poor self-management or bad attitudes. Others are diligent but simply average in academic ability.

Results: "C" students obtain mediocre or inconsistent results on tests. They have some concept of what is going on but clearly have not completely mastered the material. (Williams, 1993).

HOW TO FORM GROUPS

To divide students into four groups, use a deck of cards. Distribute them as students arrive. Announce all those with hearts form one group, clubs a second, spades and diamonds. This technique works for any size group.

Form groups according to a common element: age, gender, interest.

Randomly draw names from a hat.

Count off: if you need three groups, the first student counts 1, the next 2, the next 3, and the next begins again with 1. After each student has a number, all those with #1 form a group, #2, etc.

Let students select using any method they choose.

Use the seating pattern already established. If four students are grouped at one table, indicate they stay together as Group #1.

DID I MISS ANYTHING?

This question is frequently asked by students after missing a class. Here are some quick and quirky answers.

Nothing. When we realized you weren't here we sat with our hands folded on our desks in silence, for the full two hours.

Everything. I gave an exam worth 40 percent of the grade for this term and assigned some reading due today on which I'm about to hand out a quiz worth 50 percent.

Nothing. None of the content of this course has value or meaning. Take as many days off as you like: any activities we undertake as a class I assure you will not matter wither to you or me and are without purpose.

Everything. A few minutes after we began last time a shaft of light descended and an angel or other heavenly being appeared and revealed to us what each woman or man must do to attain divine wisdom in this life and the hereafter. This is the last time the class will meet before we disperse to bring this good news to all people on earth.

Nothing. When you are not present how could something significant occur?

Everything. Contained in this classroom is a microcosm of human existence assembled for you to query and examine and ponder. This is not the only place such an opportunity has been gathered but it was one place...and you weren't here. (Wayman, 1991).

Alibi-ography From Students

Teachers struggle to make decisions, and often feel discouraged when trying different options. You will not be able to appeal to all of the students all of the time because of different learning styles and personalities. Accept that premise and you will not be quite so surprised when students say:

> When given an objective test: "It doesn't let us express ourselves."
> When given an essay test: "It is so vague. We don't know what you expect."
> When you use the lecture format: "We don't get to participate."
> When detailed material is presented: "What's the use?

HELPING STUDENTS SUCCEED

NOTE TAKING SKILLS

BEFORE THE LECTURE

1. Read the required assignments in the textbook.
2. Review any notes taken during previous class session.
3. Write down any questions about the homework reading or assignments that you want to ask the teacher.
4. Come to class ready to take notes. Bring a binder with enough paper and a pen.
5. Sit near the front of the class to better see the board and better hear the instructor.
6. Keep a separate section in the binder for each class.
7. Get your paper ready to take notes. Draw a 2" margin on the left side of the paper.
8. Write the date and topic at the top of each page.

DURING THE LECTURE

1. Use a pen and standard 8 1/2 " x 11" paper.
2. Use only one side of the page for taking notes.
3. Write down the main ideas of the lecture on the right side of the page. Save the 2" column on the left to write down your recall clues after the lecture.
4. Write only key words and phrases; do not try to copy your teacher's exact sentences. Use an outline format and develop abbreviations.
5. Write down any examples used and copy what is visually presented by the teacher (transparencies and blackboard).
6. Write down any new terms or vocabulary the teacher defines.
7. Write neatly, it pays off by saving time in the future. Later when reviewing, make notes memorable if you are a visual learner to help you "picture" them later. Auditory learners do well to read notes out loud to help them with later recall.
8. Leave plenty of blank space between ideas so you can add missing information after asking a question.

9. Write a question mark by anything you do not understand. Ask a classmate for help later.

AFTER THE LECTURE

1. Edit your notes immediately after the lecture, revising where necessary to help you remember more facts and examples.
2. Underline the important new words and important ideas in your notes.
3. Fill in the left margin with words and phrases that briefly summarize the notes. These recall clues should be clues that will help you remember the complete information. Write additional questions in the left margin too.
4. To study for a test, cover your notes with a piece of paper, showing only the recall clues in the left margin. Read the clue and try to remember the information in the notes beside it. Then slide the paper down and check that portion to see if you remembered all the important facts.

The key principle for note taking and succeeding in the classroom is to review the notes. Simply taking the notes is not enough. Students have more positive results in their learning if they use the two step process: take good notes and *review* them.

Build in accountability for taking effective lecture notes by regularly collecting and grading them and allowing students to use their notes during exams.

EXPRESSIONS THAT FOCUS STUDENT LISTENING AND COMPREHENSION DURING LECTURES

Introductory Summaries
  Let me first explain ...
  The topic which I intend to discuss today is....
  This is important because....
  At the end of the session you will know.....
Numerical Statements
  There are two, three, etc.
Development of an Idea
  In the first place...
  Another reason is...

Contrasting Several Ideas
   On the one hand ...
   But
   However
   Although
Results of Ideas
   Therefore...
   Consequently ...
   As a result of ...
Transition of Ideas
   Turning our attention to...
   Let's think about ...
Chronology of Ideas
   First
   In the beginning
   Another
   The former
   Prior to
   Finally
Summary of Ideas
   In summary...
   In conclusion...
   As we have discussed...
   Let me review...
   For all these reasons...
As I have shown...

(Exchanges Newsletter of the California State University System Institute for Teaching and Learning, 1993).

CONSTRUCTIVE USE OF EXAMS

1. Use a variety of testing methods. Some students are better writers, some better test takers, and some better oral presenters.
2. Give feedback as promptly as possible.
3. Reduce in any way you can the threat tests pose.
4. Do not grade all tests.
5. Let students create questions for you to include on exams.

6. Do not stress the trivial.
7. Surprise quizzes and tests need to be given adequate time for students to complete.
8. Give one more exam than you usually do. For example, if you give four exams during the term, give five. Tell students they can choose any four grades. That way, if someone's goldfish dies and the student misses an exam, he or she will likely eliminate the zero from the total pool of five. This removes the teacher from being the Bad Person and trying to "judge" the tragedy of the excuse, and places the responsibility on the student where it belongs.

VS Hixson

"But I can't possibly make it to the exam that day! I've already bought tickets to South Padre Island!"

ATTENDANCE

Give students points for class participation and attendance. Do not announce the in-class activities in advance, that way students need to attend regularly to have a shot at getting the extra points. Students may feel that the small number of points accorded for their participation and attendance will not be enough to make a difference in the final grade, but you can always tell them dozens of anecdotes about borderline students whose perfect attendance records pushed them to a higher grade level.

Tell students that one-third of the final exam questions come from the lecture, not from the textbook readings. This encourages their attendance. (Geske, 1992).

MULTICULTURAL STUDENTS

- Talk with international students before or after class to help them feel more at ease in the classroom.
- If a student seems reticent to speak up in class, speak privately with him/her to discuss the situation.
- Try to eliminate idioms from class sessions.
- Write major points on the chalkboard. Also write assignments and schedules so details are not lost.
- Slow down your rate of speech, and repeat for emphasis.
- Encourage participation by telling them you are interested in hearing their viewpoints. The easiest content for English learners is related to their everyday experiences. Include opportunities for them to share their lives and culture.
- Remain patient remembering that students with language barriers often need additional time to formulate answers before speaking, and a longer time to state their answers. Provide positive encouragers like, "I'd like to hear more," or "That is interesting," or "I like the way you stated that."

ESTABLISHING RELATIONSHIPS

- Get out from behind the podium. It is always possible to move around, even in architecturally difficult classrooms. Students will follow you as you move, that keeps them active, or at least awake. You can use a lavaliere mike that moves with you, or a battery operated mike to eliminate the possibility of tripping over the cord.
- This technique helps in large classrooms, but works well in small classrooms too. Going a step further, I urge teachers to actually sit in one of the chairs among the students. This tactic really puts you in touch and

on the same level as students and diminishes the separation of power the threatening podium suggests.

STUDY SKILLS TO PASS ON TO STUDENTS

- Reading is essential and here are some ideas to help students get the most from their reading. Reading as a source of learning and remembering is a different process than reading for fun.
- Survey the entire chapter, look for the section headings and main ideas and find the topic sentence in each paragraph. Always read end of chapter summaries.
- When reading chapters, look for words that are underlined or use italics; they are likely to be important. Boldface words, or ideas set apart by numbering or lettering in lists are usually signals for the student to focus on.
- Pay attention to charts and graphs, and check out new vocabulary.
- Take notes while you are reading and use a highlight pen to notate what is important.
- After reading a section, ask yourself questions about what you have read. Outlining what has been read is another good strategy for retention. This process may appear to be time consuming. However, the effort spent while reading will make time spent reviewing more efficient.

RESPONSIBLE STUDENTS

Students have the responsibility to:

- come to every class prepared to listen, to participate, and to learn.
- read the textbook carefully, noting important ideas and rephrasing concepts in own words.
- work through the examples in the textbook, as well as the examples given in class.
- consult other students, the teacher, a tutor, and other resources whenever they need extra help.
- understand that the teacher is not principally responsible for making them understand, but that it is their job to study and to learn.

- keep an open mind and try to comprehend what the teacher is trying to get across.
- do every bit of assigned homework with proper attention and thought.
- view the teacher as a partner in education, not someone who is bent on causing them pain and frustration.
- understand that he or she is not the only student in the class, and that if he or she falls behind the class, not all questions are appropriately asked in the classroom setting. Students have the responsibility to go to the teacher's office for help.
- act as a competent adult.
- be polite and open to the teacher.
- accept that the work will be evaluated in terms of what skills any student is expected to master. (Rodell, 1994).

10 WORST STUDENT BEHAVIORS (LUDEWIG, 1994)

I find it particularly irritating when students:

1. Carry on personal conversations with others during a lecture.
2. Cheat on examinations.
3. Miss class and ask "Did I miss anything important?"
4. Place their heads on the desk or fall asleep during class.
5. Are excessively tardy.
6. Fail to read assigned textbooks or collateral materials.
7. Are absent on exam days.
8. Do not bring required materials to class.
9. Are excessively absent.
10. Miss lecture and expect the professor to provide them a personal encore.

98 THINGS YOU CAN DO THE FIRST THREE WEEKS OF CLASS (POVLACS).

Here, then, are some ideas to help you celebrate teaching and learning in your classes every term.

HELPING STUDENTS MAKE TRANSITIONS

1. Hit the ground running on the first day of class with substantial content.
2. Take attendance: roll call, clipboard, sign-in, seating chart.
3. Introduce yourself by slide, videotape, short presentation, or self-bio.
4. Hand out an informative, attractive, and user-friendly syllabus.
5. Give an assignment on the first day to be collected at the next meeting.
6. Start laboratory experiments and other exercises the first time lab meets.
7. Call attention (written and oral) to good learning habits: Completing assignments, time, previewing scheduled topics, regularly reviewing material covered, full use of time with regard for safety.
8. Give a learning style inventory to help students find out about themselves.
9. Tell students how much time they will need to study for this course.
10. Hand out supplemental study aids: library use, study tips, supplemental readings and practice exercises.
11. Explain how to study for the kind of tests you give.
12. Put in writing a limited number of ground rules regarding absence, late work, testing procedures, grading, and general decorum, and maintain these.
13. Announce office hours frequently and hold them without fail.
14. Show students how to handle learning in large classes and impersonal situations.
15. Give sample test questions; provide answers.
16. Explain the difference between legitimate collaboration and academic dishonesty: be clear when collaboration is wanted and when it is forbidden.
17. Seek out a different student each day and get to know something about him/her.
18. Find out about students' jobs: if they are working, how many hours a week, and what kinds of jobs they hold.

DIRECTING STUDENTS' ATTENTION

19. Greet students at the door when they enter the classroom.
20. Start the class on time.
21. Make a grand stage entrance touch a large class and gain attention.
22. Give a pretest on the day's topic.
23. Start the lecture with a puzzle, question, paradox, picture, or cartoon on slide or transparency to focus on the day's topic.
24. Elicit student questions and concerns at the beginning of the class and list these on the chalkboard to be answered during the hour.

25. Have students write down what they think the important issues or key points of the day's lecture will be.
26. Ask the person who is reading the student newspaper what is in the news today.

CHALLENGING THE STUDENTS

27. Have students write out their expectations for the course and their own goals for learning.
28. Use variety in methods of presentation at every class meeting.
29. Stage a figurative "coffee break" about 20 minutes into the hour: tell an anecdote, invite students to put down pens and pencils, refer to a current event, shift media.
30. Incorporate community resources; plays, concerts, the state fair, governmental agencies, businesses, the outdoors.
31. Show a film in a novel way; stop it for discussion, show a few frames only, anticipate ending, hand out a viewing or critique sheet, play and replay parts.
32. Share your philosophy of teaching with your students.
33. Form a student panel to present alternative views of the same concept.
34. Stage a change-your-mind debate, with students moving to different parts of the classroom to signal change in opinion during discussion.
35. Conduct a "living" demographic survey by having students move to different parts of the classroom: size of high school, rural vs. urban, consumer preferences.
36. Tell about your current professional interests and how you got there from your own beginnings in the discipline.
37. Conduct a role play to make a point or to lay out issues.
38. Let your students assume the role of a professional in the discipline: biologist, philosopher, literary critic, engineer, political scientist.
39. Conduct idea-generating or brainstorming sessions to expand horizons.
40. Give student two passages of material containing alternative views to compare and contrast.
41. Distribute a list of the unsolved problems, dilemmas, or great questions in your discipline and invite students to claim one as their own to investigate.
42. Ask students what books they read during the last six months.
43. Ask students what is going on in the state legislature on a subject which may affect their future.
44. Let your students see the enthusiasm you have for your subject and your love of learning.

45. Take students with you to hear guest speakers or special programs on campus.
46. Plan a "scholar-gypsy" lesson or unit which shows students the excitement of discovery in your discipline.

PROVIDING SUPPORT

47. Collect students' current telephone numbers and addresses and let them know that you may need to reach them.
48. Check out absentees. Call or write a personal note.
49. Diagnose the students' prerequisite learning by questionnaire or pretest and give them the feedback as soon as possible.
50. Hand out study questions/study guides.
51. Be redundant. Students should see, read, or hear key material at least 3 times.
52. Allow students to demonstrate progress in learning: summary quiz over the day's work, a written reaction to the day's material.
53. Use non-graded feedback to let students know how they are doing: post answers to ungraded quizzes and problem sets, do exercises in class, oral feedback.
54. Reward behavior you want: praise, stars, honor roll, personal note.
55. Use a light touch: smile, tell a good joke, break test anxiety with a sympathetic comment.
56. Organize. Give visible structure by posting the day's "menu" on chalkboard or overhead.
57. Use multiple media; overhead, slides, film, videotape, audiotape, models, sample material.
58. Make appointments with all students - individually or in small groups.
59. Use multiple examples, in multiple media, to illustrate key points and important concepts.
60. Hand out wallet-sized telephone cards with all important telephone numbers listed: office, department, resource centers, lab.
61. Print all important course dates on a card that can be handed out and taped to a mirror.
62. Eavesdrop on students before or after class and join their conversation about course topics.
63. Maintain an open gradebook, with grades kept current so that students can check their progress.
64. Check to see if any students are having problems with any academic or campus matters and direct those who are to appropriate offices or resources.

65. Tell students what they need to do to receive an "A" in your course.
66. Stop the world to find out what your students are thinking, feeling, and doing in their everyday lives.

ENCOURAGING ACTIVE LEARNING

67. Have students write something regularly: journal entries, course commentaries, content reports.
68. Invite students to critique each other's essays or short answers on tests for readability or content.
69. Invite students to ask questions frequently.
70. Probe student responses to questions and their comments.
71. Put students into pairs or "learning cells" to quiz each other over material for the day.
72. Give students an opportunity to voice opinions about the subject matter.
73. Have students apply subject matter to solve real problems.
74. Give students red, yellow, and green cards (made of posterboard) and periodically call for a vote on an issue by asking for a simultaneous show of cards.
75. Roam the aisles of your classroom and carry on running conversations with students as they work on course problems.
76. Gather student feedback in first three weeks to improve teaching and learning.
77. Ask a question directed to one student and wait for an answer.
78. Place a suggestion box in the rear of the room and encourage students to make written comments every time the class meets.
79. Do oral, show-of-hands, multiple choice tests for summary, review, and instant feedback.
80. Use task groups to accomplish specific objectives.
81. Grade quizzes and exercises in class as a learning tool.
82. Give students plenty of opportunity for practice before a major test.
83. Give a test early in the term and return it graded at the next class meeting.
84. Have students write questions on index cards to be collected and answered the next class period.
85. Make collaborative assignments for several students to work on together.
86. Assign written paraphrases and summaries of difficult reading.
87. Appoint a student volunteer weekly to ask "dumb questions" for other class members.
88. Give students a take-home problem relating to the day's lecture.
89. Encourage students to bring current news items to class which relate to the subject matter and post these on a bulletin board nearby.

90. Practice allowing sufficient "wait time" when posing questions.

BUILDING COMMUNITY

91. Use special techniques to help you learn names.
92. Set up a buddy system or helping trios.
93. Find out about your students via questions on an index card.
94. Take pictures of students (snapshots in small groups/mugshots) and post in classroom, office, or lab.
95. Form small groups for getting acquainted, mix and form new groups several times.
96. Assign a team project early in the term and provide time to assemble the team.
97. Solicit suggestions from students for outside resources and guest speakers on course topics.
98. Exchange a tip for successful teaching with a colleague.

Adapted from Joyce T. Povlacs, The University of Nebraska, Lincoln Teaching and Learning Center

The ideas in this chapter were presented in a way to provide you quick and easy reference. Humor was inserted to keep you reading and interested until the end. This is almost the end.

Ever wonder why pretzels are made in a loose-knot pattern?

Invented by medieval monks as rewards for children learning their holy lessons, pretzels were shaped to represent a pair of arms folded in prayer across a child's chest. (Smith, 1991 & 1994).

You deserve a pretzel for having worked through this book. This is the end for me, but a beginning for some of you, and a continuation for many others of an ongoing commitment to educational excellence. Complete puzzle.

ELEVEN ELEMENTS FOR EDUCATIONAL EXCELLENCE

ACROSS

1. to possess skill and knowledge in an area acquired through <u>experience</u>

2. to gain recognition and acceptance

3. to secure cooperation and create an <u>environment</u>

4. to put plan into action and operate efficiently

5. to have strong <u>excitement</u>, fervor, zeal and <u>enjoyment</u>

6. to give authority to those you teach, to <u>encourage</u> and <u>enrich</u>

7. to judge what was done and make decisions on what to do before you <u>exit</u>

DOWN

1. to mark the beginning of a teaching profession

2. to gather data and assess what needs to be done, to discover <u>expectations</u>

4. to have a dynamic <u>exertion</u> of power

6. to teach others and facilitate learning

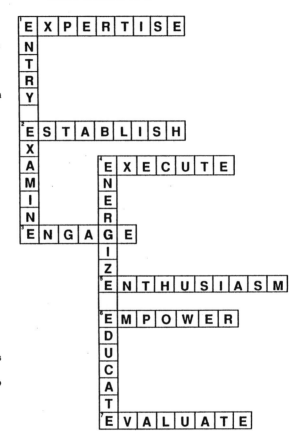

REFERENCES

American Association for Higher Education Bulletin. (1993, November). Students on faculty. 18-19.

Bach, R. (1970). *Jonathan Livingston Seagull*. New York: Macmillan.

Barrows, H. S. (1988). *The Tutorial Process*. Springfield, IL: Southern Illinois University School of Medicine.

Bateson, M. C. (1989). *Composing A Life*. Atlantic Monthly Press.

Beidler, P. G. (1984, November). Why teach?. *Alumni Magazine Consortium*, Baltimore: Johns Hopkins University, 1-4.

Bloom, B. S. (Ed.) (1956). Englehart, M. D., Furst, E. J., Hill, W. H., & Krathwohl, D. R. *Taxonomy of Educational Objectives: Handbook I, Cognitive Domain*. New York: D. McKay.

Bonwell, C. (1991). The enhanced lecture. Center for Teaching and Learning, Southeast Missouri State University.

Brookfield, S. (1986). *Understanding and Facilitating Adult Learning*. San Francisco: Jossey-Bass.

Canfield, J. & Hansen, M. (1996). *3rd Serving of Chicken Soup for the Soul*. Deerfield, FL: Health Communications, Inc.

Cartwright, L. J. (1993, August/September). Practical techniques for integrating humor in the classroom. *The Teaching Professor*, 7,(7), 7.

Chickering, A. W. & Gamson, Z. F. (1987, June). Seven Principles for Good Practice in Undergraduate Education. *The Wingspread Journal*, 9,(2), 1.

Chiodo, J. J. (1989). Professors who fail may be our best teachers. *Teacher Education Quarterly, 16*, 79-83.

Collins, M. L. (1976). "Enthusiasm Rating Chart" Adapted from Practical Applications of Research, PHI DELTA KAPPA Newsletter, June 1981.

Conti, G. (1990). Identifying your teaching style. In M. W. Galbraith (Ed.), Adult Learning Methods: a guide for effective instruction. Malabar, FL: Krieger Publishing Co.

Cross, K. P. (1981). *Adults As Learners*. San Francisco: Jossey-Bass.

Curry, J. J. (1991). The Facilitator's Guide to the Small Group Process. (Unpublished). p. 11.

Dead Poets Society. (1989). Touchstone Pictures.

278   Kay F. Quam

Educating Rita. (1984). Columbia Pictures. Acorn Pictures.

Elias, J. & Merriam, S. (1980*). Philosophical foundations of adult education.* Malabar, FL: Robert E. Krieger Publishing Co.

Elias, J.& Merriam, S. (1995) *Philosophical foundations of adult education* Malabar, FL: Robert E. Krieger Publishing Co.(2nd ed.)

Exchanges Newsletter of the California State University System Institute for Teaching and Learning, (1993, Fall). *5*,(1).

Fisch, L. (1988). The case for leaving things out. *Connexions, 1*,(3).

Flanner, D. & Wistock R. (1991, June). Why we do what we do: Our working philosophy of adult education. *Adult Learning*, 7-8.

Foley, R. & Smilansky, J. (1980). *Teaching techniques: A handbook for health professionals.* McGraw-Hill, Inc.

Garcia, R. (1991, October). Twelve ways of looking at a blackboard. *The Teaching Professor.* 5,(8), 5-6.

Geske, J. (1992). Overcoming the drawbacks of the large lecture class, *College Teaching, 40,(*4), 151-154.

Grasha, A. & Riechmann, S. (1972*). Student Learning Styles Questionnaire.* Paper presented at the Adult Education Conference, Cincinnati, OH, October, 1988.

Gronlund, N. E. (1995). *How to write and use instructional objectives.* Merrill: Englewood Cliffs, New Jersey.

Hadley, H.N. (1975). Educational Orientation Questionnaire. Personal Communication.

Johnson, R. E. & Burns, E. A. (1983, May). *The boring conference presentation: How to do it better yourself.* Paper presented at the meeting of the Society of Teachers of Family Medicine, Boston.

King, A. (1993). From sage on the stage to guide on the side. *College Teaching, 41*,(1), 30-35.

Knowles, M. S. (1970). *The modern practice of adult education.* New York: Association Press.

Kolb, D. A. (1976). Learning-Style Inventory: Technical Manual. Boston: McBer & Co.

Krathwohl, D. R., Bloom, B. S., & Masia, B. B. (1964). *Taxonomy of Educational Objectives: Handbook II, Affective Domain.* New York: D. McKay.

Kurfiss, J. G. (1988). Critical Thinking: Theory, Research, Practice and Possibilities, ASHE-ERIC Higher Education Report No. 2, Washington, DC Association for the Study of Higher Education, 111-113.

Loughary, J. W. & Hopson, B. (1979). *Producing workshops, seminars, and short courses: A trainer's handbook.* Chicago: Follett.

Ludewig, L. M. (1993, April). Student perceptions of instructor behaviors. *The Teaching Professor, 7*,(4), 1.

Ludewig, L. M. (1994, May). 10 worst student behaviors. *The Teaching Professor, 8*,(5), 2.

McDougle, L. G. (1981). Teaching hints for training instructors. *Supervisor,* 14-17.

McGee, P. E. & Goldstein, J. H. (Eds.) (1983*). Handbook of humor research.* New York: Springer-Verlog.

McKeachie, (1974). The decline and fall of the laws of learning. *Educational Researcher, 3* (3), 7-11.

Medical College of Wisconsin (1985). Department of Family Practice Newsletter, *1*,(5).

Meyers, C. & Jones, T. B. (1993). *Promoting active learning: Strategies for the college classroom.* San Francisco: Jossey-Bass.

Miller, H. L. (1964). *Teaching and learning in adult education.* New York: MacMillan.

Poulacs, Joyce T. "98 Things You Can Do The First Three Weeks of Class" The University of Nebraska, Lincoln, Teaching and Learning Center.

Quam, K. F. (1992*). Facilitator guide.* Lombard, IL. National College of Chiropractic.

Rankin, J. A. (1993, March). Preparing medical libraries for use by students in PBL curricula. *Academic Medicine, 68*(3), 205-206.

Rezler, A. G. & Rezmovic, V. (1981, February). The learning preference inventory. *The Journal of Allied Health*, 28-34.

Robinson, R. (1979). *An introduction to helping adults learn and change.* Milwaukee, WI: Omnibook Co.

Rodell, L. M. (1994, January). Math anxiety bill of responsibilities. *The Teaching Professor, 8*,(1) 3.

Sandy, W. (1990). *Forging the productivity partnership.* McGraw Hill.

Schlesinger, R. (1992). Presentation at ISETA Conference, San Pedro, CA. Taken from *The Warmup Manual Volume II*, Toronto: Nell Warren Associates, Inc.

Schmidt, H. G., Van Der Arend A., Moust J. H. C. et al. (1993, October). Influence of tutors' subject-matter expertise on student effort and achievement in problem-based learning. *Academic Medicine, 68*,(10), 784-791.

INDEX

field trips, 46, 81, 83, 119, 189
Focus Discussion, 183
force-field analysis, 9

G

Grade Expectations, 260
Group Discussion, 107, 121, 145, 146,
 147, 148
Groups, How To Form, 261

H

hand gestures, 223
hands-on exercises, 46, 192
Heuristic, 46
Hostile Group, 153
humor, 230, 231, 251, 274, 280

I

Individual learning, 117
Individual Self-Actualization, 32
information gathering, 49
Intellectual Development, 32, 73
introductions in groups, ideas for
 conducting, 160
Irrelevant Comments, 152

K

kinesics, 223
Kinesthetic or Haptic, 50

L

Lagging Discussion, 152
Learning efficiency, 49
Learning Preference Inventory, 51
Learning Styles, 49, 51, 53, 61, 278
Learning Styles, Types of, 51

lecture method, 120, 168, 175, 194
Left brain teachers, 51
Limit Participation, 183

M

Mnemonics, 55
Modality Strengths, 63
motivation, 3, 4, 7, 18, 48, 51, 73, 80, 85,
 86, 89, 199
mugshots, 274
Multicultural Students, vii, 267

N

nonwords, 225
Note Taking Skills, vii, 263

O

Overhead transparencies, 236, 237

P

participation criteria, 162
participation, levels of, 80, 85, 88
Performance Outcomes, 129
Philosophy of Adult Education Inventory
 (PAEI), 16
piggy backing, 120
positive attitude, 82, 86
Practical Problem Solving, 32
presentations, xii, 82, 217, 231, 232, 234
prior learning, 35
Problem-based Learning, 80
Problem-Based Learning (PBL), 7, 187,
 188, 189, 191, 192, 193, 195, 196, 197,
 198, 199, 201, 202, 203, 204, 205, 207,
 279, 280
Problem-solving group, 117